# T&T CLARK STUDY GUIDES TO THE OLD TESTAMENT

## JEREMIAH

*Series Editor*
Adrian Curtis, University of Manchester, UK
Published in Association with the Society for Old Testament Study

# JEREMIAH

# An Introduction and Study Guide
## Prophecy in a Time of Crisis

By
**Mary E. Mills**

Bloomsbury T&T Clark
An imprint of Bloomsbury Publishing Plc

B L O O M S B U R Y
LONDON · OXFORD · NEW YORK · NEW DELHI · SYDNEY

**Bloomsbury T&T Clark**

An imprint of Bloomsbury Publishing Plc

Imprint previously known as T&T Clark

50 Bedford Square
London
WC1B 3DP
UK

1385 Broadway
New York
NY 10018
USA

**www.bloomsbury.com**

**BLOOMSBURY, T&T CLARK and the Diana logo are trademarks of
Bloomsbury Publishing Plc**

First published 2015. This edition published 2017

**British Library Cataloguing-in-Publication Data**
A catalogue record for this book is available from the British Library.

ISBN: PB: 978-0-5676-7105-9
ePDF: 978-0-5676-7106-6
ePub: 978-0-5676-7107-3

**Library of Congress Cataloging-in-Publication Data**
A catalog record for this book is available from the Library of Congress.

Series: T&T Clark Study Guides to the Old Testament, volume 20

Cover design: clareturner.co.uk

Typeset by Newgen Knowledge Works (P) Ltd., Chennai, India

# Contents

# ABBREVIATIONS

| | |
|---|---|
| *CBQ* | *Catholic Biblical Quarterly* |
| CEB | Common English Bible |
| GNB | Good News Bible |
| JB | *Jerusalem Bible* |
| *JBL* | *Journal of Biblical Literature* |
| *JSOT* | *Journal for the Study of the Old Testament* |
| KJV | King James Version |
| LXX | Septuagint |
| MT | Masoretic Text |
| NEB | New English Bible |
| NIV | New International Version |
| NJB | New Jerusalem Bible |
| NRSV | New Revised Standard Version |
| OAN | Oracles against the Nations |
| RB | Revised Bible |
| RSV | Revised Standard Version |

## Chapter 1

## INTRODUCTION

This study guide approaches the task of interpreting the book of Jeremiah through an exploration of the successive ways of reading the text generated by modern biblical studies. It does so because looking at the history of interpretation demonstrates how a book, which has a given set of chapters and literary content, gives rise to multiple meanings. Jeremiah is a book which is introduced as the record of Jeremiah's oracles but which also contains material relating to his career and which ends with a chapter describing the fall of Jerusalem, presented by the narrator of the entire work. Within this framework the book contains disparate literary styles: oracles, sermons, narratives and autobiographical speech. The possible unity of meaning within the book of Jeremiah is constantly fragmented by the shift between these different literary forms.

Academic writers of the twentieth and twenty-first centuries acknowledged this basic reality about the text of Jeremiah while also seeking to establish who the author or editors of the book were and how events reported in Jeremiah relate to historical events. Literary critics in their turn focused on the poetics of the book, on how metaphor, poetry, prose and symbolism all help to shape its message. Historical, literary and theological interpretations of Jeremiah cannot be separated from investigating the prophet himself as he is presented in this biblical work. Whether as historical person, literary character, or representative of a religio-social teaching, Jeremiah dominates the book named after him. This introduction to interpreting the book of Jeremiah will examine all of these prophetic profiles, structuring this investigation of the biblical book and its meaning in accordance with the findings of successive waves of scholarship in modern biblical studies in the twentieth and twenty-first centuries.

Before embarking on an exploration of the modern reception of Jeremiah, the guide focuses attention on the importance of engaging in a close reading of the biblical text in order to be able to understand and apply the various interpretive strategies employed by scholars to read Jeremiah. The first phase of this scholarly interpretation was concerned with what lay behind the text, its historical origins and early shape, especially author, date and provenance. A further phase of study examined the contents of the book in their own right, investigating the rhetorical structure of texts. These stages of study led to exploration of the issue of how the text of Jeremiah seeks to make an impact on readers and on how readers engage with the material—the audience in front of the text. The guide follows this chronological advance of scholarship across the twentieth and twenty-first centuries.

It was historical issues behind the text which first dominated the interpretation of Jeremiah in modern times. The foundational work of Bernhard Duhm (1901) established the possibility of three sources which combined to produce the final book, the earliest of which was the sayings of an historical prophet, Jeremiah. This hypothesis has formed the basis for much later work on the book of Jeremiah and led to the growth of the view that the corpus of Jeremiah tradition was subject in antiquity to a rolling process of expansions, as fresh audiences sought meaning for their time within the traditional material. A major resource for exploring the compositional history of the book of Jeremiah is found in the comparison of texts of the book in different ancient language versions. The Masoretic Hebrew version is longer than that of the Greek Septuagint version, which makes possible discussions of how an earlier form of the materials was added to over time, within antiquity. This matter is discussed further in Chapter 3 below.

By the 1980s new methodologies for reading Jeremiah were emerging. This change in focus involved a move from examination of what lies 'behind the text', its historical origins and purpose, to what is found 'in the text', the manner in which the book constructs its message, its use of metaphor, poetry, prose. In this methodology the book of Jeremiah is read as a piece of literature, with its own symbolic world shaped by plot, characterization and place and time settings. This approach has produced commentaries which examine in depth the rhetorical structure of Jeremiah and its impact on readers. A focus on literary genres has opened out in recent study to comparison with contemporary literary styles such as fantasy and horror. Giving attention to readership has led to consideration of reading the text from the perspectives of women and postcolonial cultures. There has been a movement away from the focus on temporality as a tool for interpreting text and the introduction of spatiality as a parallel reading tool. It is not just the dating of composition of particular sections of the book which counts but also the locations—cultural and physical—of different readership groups.

The development of Jeremiah studies away from historical issues was led by the Society of Biblical Literature Programme Unit on the Composition of Jeremiah and owes a great deal to the leadership of Pete Diamond. Moving from questions of what might lie behind the text, this school of thought stressed what is in the text, the way in which the text performs its task as literature—what can be called the study of textual rhetoric. The rhetorical perspective acknowledges the individual contribution of sub-units of material to the book as a whole and to the way the book performs its message. It is, for example, possible to view the passages in Jeremiah labelled by scholars 'the confessions of the prophet' (see Chapter 2 below) as having an apologetic purpose when viewed from within chaps. 1–25. This defence of divine engagement in militaristic imperialism at the expense of the home community constructs a message of judgement on the leadership of Judah in the time of kings.

The circle of scholars who have taken this literary methodology forward include Louis Stulman and Kathleen O'Connor, both of whom have studied in detail the emphasis in Jeremiah on social and political fragmentation, on terror and pain. Their reading style looks back to the earlier work of Timothy Polk on the prophetic persona and the 'imagined' figure of the prophet in this biblical book. From an exploration of the literary style of Jeremiah scholarship has moved out to the nature of the audiences whose reading of the text gives life to words on a page, especially in regard to feminist and post-colonial readings. Words and ideas emerge from and make sense in particular communities of readers. What an audience gains from an act of reading is related to where it starts from; this applies as much to ancient audiences as to modern ones but also to every generation of readers. Where readers are located is of central significance.

A third strand of interpretive methodology is found in a synchronic reading of the book which leads to the proposition of an overall theological meaning for the work. The theological approach has been furthered in the work of Walter Brueggemann whose readings of the prophet provide the basis for the forms of pastoral theology which he offers pastoral ministers in their work of preaching and teaching the congregation. His foundational study of the prophetic imagination, in two volumes, bring out the paired emotions of despair and optimism, the collapse of a familiar cultural setting and the reconstruction of tradition which communicates with a new social context.

In summary, the field of Jeremiah studies contains a number of parallel strands all of which refer back to the original language versions of the book. In the development of scholarly commentary the primacy of historical research has gradually been eroded and the way opened up for reading methodologies which address the interests of readers from a number of modern social locations. All reading methodologies acknowledge the somewhat fragmentary nature of the primary text but whereas historical research seeks to explain how that state came to be, rhetorical interests pursue the literary devices by which such fragmentation operates within the final form of the book.

Broadly speaking the insights produced by these several styles of interpretation provide meanings which range from the particular message of a single passage to the over-arching strategy of the canonical book, as this is found in the Masoretic canon of the Hebrew Bible. Scholarship identified the presence of individual sources within the book in line with shifts from one literary style to another, such as from poetry to prose and in the use of clear formula such as 'thus says the Lord' as a marker of a new prophetic oracle within the poetic collection of chaps. 1–25. The presence of so-called 'temple sermons', as in chap. 7, identified a specific style within the prose material which scholars noted as having similarities with the style of Deuteronomy. The 'Oracles against the Nations' [OANs], which occur later in chaps. 4–51 of the book, share a common format and some content with parallel passages in the other two major prophets and so form a separate collection which has been set into the edited book of Jeremiah. The origins and dating of such individual units of material has been a major interest for historical criticism.

At the same time rhetorical scholarship has revealed the commonality of mood across much of Jeremiah: a symbolic universe of destabilization, of 'terror all around', in which the status quo of Jerusalemite elite culture founded on temple/palace connections is contested and denounced—as found in Jeremiah's dispute with Hananiah (chap. 28). The use of female iconography to identify false worship and idolatry has offered feminist scholarship the opportunity to critique a simple acceptance of the book's message by modern audiences since a feminist approach suggests that use of female metaphors negativizes the role and status of women in society. Vivid imagery of scenes of military invasion and defeat provide material for exploring the use of the grotesque as a form of political satire, while postcolonial readers may look away from the book's focus on Jerusalem to the literary role of marginal places/spaces such as Egypt and Babylon in the construction of meaning.

It is clear that Jeremiah is a composite text when looked at both historically and from the angle of the literary styles of which it is composed, but it now forms a single book within the canonical collection of written prophecy. The modern reader receives the contents of Jeremiah on the level of synchronicity, being able to read the final form of the text at a single encounter. Hence both temporal and spatial axes are relevant to understanding and interpreting the book. In terms of the history of composition, readers can take the text apart to research the literary elements of which it is composed and consider how these smaller pieces were put together in the process of editing, while reading through the text as a whole leads to a focus on the manner in which text manages meaning: the roles of plot, characters and scene-settings as part of a spatial poetics which sets out a symbolic narrative universe.

In the construction of this literary world, Judah, Egypt and Babylon perform the symbolic function of expressing viewpoints which are essentially forms of political theology. The book of Jeremiah provides a way to examine everyday reality through the lens of religious tradition from a Judahite angle. Jeremiah is a character who appears to be ambivalent about the values of his own local royal government of which he is a central player. He wants to support his fellow citizens and yet condemns their practices. His message is ambivalent also about Babylon which he views both as a necessary overlord and as a foreign invader whose power will in future be destroyed. Jeremiah preaches to the exiles of Judah who flee to Egypt but is at the same time uncertain that their way of life will bring benefits to them.

If one essential question about Jeremiah is who or what this prophet was and what that has to do with a book described as his work, this study guide suggests how many different viewpoints and debates the two simple questions of who and what the prophet was can generate. To what extent does a modern reader engage the historical events of antiquity when reading Jeremiah? Is it the case that the reader encounters only a literary rendering of how past events are being transmitted to a later readership? If the prophet's task is speech-in-action how far can a work of literature be regarded as a prophetic work, as Stuart Weeks, for instance, has asked? Whether understood as a chronicle or as a direct address to a living readership, the book of Jeremiah is closely concerned with divine control of everyday life—politics and wars. It can be asked, what images of God emerge from such a work of political theology.

## Further Reading/References

Each of the following chapters of this introduction to Jeremiah ends with a short bibliography of works referred to in that chapter which can be consulted for further reading about the topics addressed in the chapter.

The introductory chapter is a good place to list major commentaries on Jeremiah since these are reference works which a reader can consult whenever in-depth information is needed with regard to a particular verse or passage of the biblical book. Although the commentary is a reference work, each volume is shaped both by the intentions of the respective publishing house and the views of the individual scholar. It is useful, therefore, to read the foreword or preface to a commentary before investigating what it has to say about details of the ancient text.

*Selected major works of commentary*
Duhm, B.
  1901   *Das Buch Jeremia* (Tübingen: Mohr).
Herrmann, S.
  1986   *Jeremia* (Bern: Peter Lang Verlag).
Weeks, Stuart
  2008   'Jeremiah as a prophetic book'. in Hans Barstad and Reinhard Kratz (eds.), *Prophecy in the Book of Jeremiah* (Berlin: De Gruyter), pp. 265-74.

*English Language Commentaries*

Allen, L.
  2008   *Jeremiah* (Louisville, KY: Westminster/John Knox Press).
Berrigan, D.
  1999   *Jeremiah: The World; The Wound of God* (Augsburg: Fortress Press).
Boadt, L.
  1982   *Jeremiah 1–25/Jeremiah 26–52, Habbakuk, Zephaniah, Nahum* (Wilmington, DE: Michael Glazier).
Brueggemann, W.
  1998   *A Commentary on Jeremiah: Exile and Homecoming* (Grand Rapids, MI: Eerdmans).
Carroll, R.
  1986   *Jeremiah: A Commentary* (London: SCM Press).
Clements, R.
  1988   *Jeremiah: A Commentary for Teaching and Preaching* (Louisville, KY: Westminster/John Knox Press).
Fretheim, T.
  2002   *Jeremiah* (Macon, GA: Smyth & Helwys).
Holladay, W.
  1986   *Jeremiah*, Vol. 1 (Philadelphia: Fortress Press).
  1989   *Jeremiah*, Vol. 2 (Minneapolis: Fortress Press).
Hyatt, J.
  1956   'The Book of Jeremiah: Introduction and Exegesis', *The Interpreter's Bible* (New York: Abingdon Press).
Jones, D.
  1992   *Jeremiah* (Grand Rapids, MI: Eerdmans).
Leslie, E.
  1954   *Jeremiah: Chronologically Arranged, Translated and Interpreted* (New York: Abingdon Press).
Longman, Tremper III
  2008   *Jeremiah, Lamentations* (Grand Rapids, MI: Baker Academic).
Lundbom, J.
  2007   *Jeremiah 21–36* (New Haven, CT: Yale University Press).
McKane, W.
  1986   *Jeremiah*, Vol. 1 (Edinburgh: T. & T. Clark).
  1996   *Jeremiah*, Vol. 2 (Edinburgh: T. & T. Clark).
McKeating, H.
  1998   *The Book of Jeremiah* (London: Epworth Press).
McKeown, J., P. Scalise and T. Smothers
  1995   *Jeremiah 26–52* (Waco, TX: Word Press).
Mowinckel, S.
  1914   *Zur Komposition des Buches Jeremia* (Oslo: Jacob Dybwad).
Nicholson, E.
  1973   *The Book of the Prophet Jeremiah* (2 vols.; Cambridge: Cambridge University Press).
Stulman, L.
  2005   *Jeremiah* (Nashville: Abingdon Press).
Thompson, J.
  1980   *The Book of Jeremiah* (Grand Rapids, MI: Eerdmans).

In addition it will be useful to the reader to have an overview of the history of ancient Israel. This is a much debated topic among scholars and no single account can cover the issues about historicity which have been raised to the biblical account of Israel's origins and experiences, found in the Torah (Pentateuch) and Prophets.

However, a useful work for those who have little grasp of the basic chronology into which the accounts of the late monarchy fit is to found in:

Liverani, M., trans. P. Davies and C. Peri
  2003   *Israel's History and the History of Israel* (London: Equinox).

For reflections on the nature of prophecy and prophets at this time see:

Grabbe, L.
  1995   *Priests, Prophets, Diviners, Sages: Socio-historical Study of Religious Specialists in Ancient Israel* (Valley Forge, PA: Trinity Press International).

Chapter 2

## READING THE BOOK OF JEREMIAH

In his study guide of the 1980s Robert Carroll urged students of the book
of Jeremiah to spend time reading the work for themselves and working
out its contents from a close reading of the biblical text. This chapter will
follow that advice by laying out the book of Jeremiah as it is encountered
by the one who reads from chap. 1 to chap. 52. It should be remembered
that chapter and verse divisions were added to the text long after its original
form, for the convenience of scholars in citing particular passages for discussion. Although these divisions are generally reasonable differentiations
of subunits of material, such as a move from poetry to prose, they do not
have authority to impose meaning on the book, whose meaning is shaped
by internal literary features: units of text with their own starting point, mood
and conclusion.

Likewise it is to be remembered that the oldest versions of the book were
written in ancient languages, Hebrew and Greek, and that the English language version of the material has had to seek out translations which provide a working equivalence with the original, since all languages have their
own structures and idioms. In addition, English Bible editions translate the
same original with different English phrasing depending on the purpose the
editors of the edition had in mind. It is very helpful, therefore, to consult at
least two separate English editions of the Bible and to compare and contrast
the translations of Jeremiah in each edition.

The Revised Standard Version (RSV), for example, sets out to be a study
edition and so keeps close to the shape of the ancient versions even when
this makes for clumsy or strange English wording. The Good News Bible
(GNB), written for those who speak English but who do not have a detailed
grasp of the language, tends to suppress the complexities of the original versions and also to use simple English expressions to convey the basic meaning of the biblical material. When using an English edition of Jeremiah,
then, it is helpful to read the editors' Preface to find out what type of audience they had in mind as this will have coloured their translation practices.

The following schema offers a guide for reading the book through carefully and can be used as a framework for making notes on the specific contents of each subsection of material. The first chapter of any book usually

sets the scene for the material which is to follow. Reading the initial chapter carefully indicates the nature of later content and this is no different with Jeremiah. Chapter 1 offers an editorial comment followed by a story concerning the origins and authority of the oracles which follow. This material introduces the topic of destruction which is pursued in chaps. 1–25.

Jeremiah 1.1-3 contains the editors' overall comment on the contents of the book and provides an historical link for the material which follows in the first 25 chapters. One question to ask is 'what is the impact of setting the work of the prophet in this way?' What sort of information does it provide about the origins of the prophecies and the profile of Jeremiah himself? Jeremiah 1.4-10 recounts the call of the prophet. It is significant that this passage appears as an autobiographical account which dramatizes the close relation of humanity and God, making the prophet a messenger, a mouthpiece for divine perspectives on society. Jeremiah 1.11-19 adds to the message about Jeremiah set out in vv. 4-10, giving more detail about the prophetic task and the events which God is planning, stressing the destruction which is planned and which the prophet must proclaim and by proclaiming bring into being. At the same time the addition in v. 10 of the phrase 'to build and to plant' foreshadows chaps. 30–31 with their message of reconstruction following collapse.

In the chapters of the main part of the book, poetic and prose sections of material play out these interpretations of public affairs in many individual units of text, mainly with the message of doom. The following account of the contents of Jeremiah breaks down chaps. 2–52 into smaller sections, each of which has its own contribution to the overall theme. This account of the book's contents is provided to encourage readers to move slowly through Jeremiah, reading each section of material closely, in order to identify subunits and their particular contributions to the overall message of the book. This is a central skill to acquire in order to work successfully with the succeeding chapters of this guide.

Jeremiah 2–6 contains many individual poetic oracles regarding Judah/ Jerusalem, each introduced as the Word of the Lord to the prophet. The reader can work out where each unit starts/stops and analyse how it builds up a picture of judgment and doom. For example Jer. 2.1 introduces an oracle with the phrase 'the word of the Lord…thus says'. This runs till the end of v. 3 ['says the Lord']. Verse 4 starts another individual oracle which runs till v. 8.

Chapter 7 is marked by the switch from poetry to prose. This chapter introduces the genre of prose sermon, a style which repeats in the succeeding chapters. These prose sermons have their own style and should be read as individual passages within the book. The reader should explore the interweaving of the themes of temple and covenant in this sermon and its companions. There is a similarity of tone—reliance on the temple site as proof of safety is an illusion—and historical examples drawn from Israel's past history are brought in to prove this point.

Chapters 8–10 build up the atmosphere of doom for Judah through an alternation of poetic oracles and prose passages. Chapter 8, for instance, starts with a prose account of the fate of kings which opens up into poetic oracles in v. 4. The oracles talk more widely of wicked people and uses nature imagery—the metaphor of horse and stork—to make its point. Chapter 11 repeats messages of doom but also adds in the material labelled by scholars as Jeremiah's Confessions: passages where the prophet speaks of his suffering at first hand.

See here Jer. 11.18-20, for instance. In this passage the narrator tells of a conversation between God and prophet where Jeremiah agrees to preach an evil future for Judah. This is followed by poetic material which identifies a plot against the messenger and the prophet speaks as himself, 'I'. He begs God for support in this time of attack. Chapter 12 continues this theme with the prophet's lament over his own fate of having to speak negatively and so incurring the wrath of citizens as an assault on his own person. This motif repeats in the other Confession passages where Jeremiah becomes increasingly distressed by his isolation from his fellow citizens and comes to feel abandoned by the deity whose message he carries.

So far the book has been concerned with words, the Word of the Lord which must be spoken but chap. 13 adds a further element to the book whereby the prophet is required to perform symbolic actions in pursuit of his proclamation of judgment. Further examples of prophetic acts occur later in the book. In this instance the focus of the action is on a linen strip which can be used as clothing. The prophet wears it, buries it and then unearths it to find that it has become useless for its purpose. This provides an allegorical event since the cloth signifies the nation. Just as a person throws away a ruined garment so God will abandon the people.

In linking prophetic speech with prophetic act as two means of conveying a single message there is a close alignment of the use of the mouth with that of the hands and the whole body. It is important to remember that the translation 'word' for Hebrew *dabar* tells only a part of the original Hebrew meaning—which includes acts, events and things. Consider how the experience of being a prophet draws in the entire bodily existence—the power of rational understanding and speech, the treatment of the body, the links between individual and family. See here chap. 16, with its prohibition of a normal family life.

Chapter 24 initiates a new stage in the chronological shaping of the Jeremiah material and chaps. 24–27 contain temporal markers to situate Jeremiah's work. They indicate prophecy at the time of the initial exile, dated by the reign of Jehoiachin. The tone of this is positive towards the Babylonian exiles and negative to Zedekiah and the government which remained in Judah. Chapter 25 speaks of 70 years of captivity for those who become captives as a result of failing to listen to Jeremiah's message, after which God will defeat Babylon too. Chapter 26 marks a change to prose narratives which tell of threats which were offered to Jeremiah on account of his message, while chap. 27 repeats the message that Judah is destined to be subordinated to Babylonian rule.

Within this symbolic world of prophecy and rejection a particular case study emerges in chap. 28 which provides an example of the conflict between true and false prophecy as found in biblical prophetic literature. The prophet in each major book of prophecy faces opposition from religious authorities but his message prevails and the death of the opponent is foretold. This style is found also in the book of Amos chap. 7 for example. Here the focus is on a contest between Jeremiah and Hananiah in which each man performs similar acts to prove the point he is making.

Hananiah refers to the Babylonian power as a yoke of oppression which he says God will break and free the kingdom. Jeremiah counters his opponent by wearing a yoke on his neck to assert his view that Babylonian power is pre-destined by God. Hananiah symbolically breaks Jeremiah's wooden yoke to prove his is the more powerful prophecy but Jeremiah scoffs that God will replace wood with iron—a yoke which cannot be broken. He makes his point by foretelling Hananiah's own death, an event which is then referred to in the last verse of the chapter. It is clear that the dispute is not simply a matter of religious ideals but is involved with state policy. Each prophet represents a court faction, whether for a foreign policy of war or peace: conspiracy to rebel against the overlord or to submit to the empire. Both men appeal to the same deity as the author of their message and there is no obvious difference in their methods of action.

Chapters 30–31 mark a main thematic change since the oracles set out their move to the theme of restoration after suffering. The return from exile is offered as a future hope of restoration to land ownership and a time of peace and prosperity. This language of return and rebuilding is the second phase of prophecy found in all the prophetic books whose earlier literary contents are contextualized as belonging to the period before local kingdoms are overrun by foreign armies—the pre-exilic phase of their history. It raises questions about dating and whether a prophet whose main task is denunciation could historically have switched mood so fully. Here in Jeremiah a link between judgment and restoration is made though the theme of covenant broken and then restored.

Chapters 32–44 contain what has been labelled the Prose Narratives. The gaze returns from the distant future to Jeremiah's lifetime and the events of his career at court. The chapters engage in a prose chronicle style where events and prophecies are fitted into specific royal reigns and Jeremiah's part in this is described sometimes by an outside narrator. Embedded into the narrative are first person speeches made by the prophet and other key players. In chap. 38 Jeremiah is thrown into a pit from which he only just escapes with his life as a result of intervention by supporters at court. This event continues the thematic mood of earlier material in which the prophet is surrounded by controversy. Chapter 36 contains an account of a scroll which the prophet wrote and the king burned; is the scroll meant to be a copy of the book of Jeremiah? The passage raises a further question in that it refers to Jeremiah's scribe or secretary, Baruch. This literary figure has become the focus for much scholarly discussion. Chapter 39 depicts the fall of Jerusalem and the captivity of Jeremiah. He is, however, freed and then relates to a group of refugees who flee to Egypt, for whom also he prophesies.

At this point the narrative breaks off and chaps. 46–51 provide a mostly poetic series of Oracles against the Nations—Philistines, Moab, Ammon, Edom, Babylon. These oracles form a separate section of the book since they concern other nations than the home community of Judah. They are undated and after the initial attribution to Jeremiah in chap. 46.1 are anonymous oracles. However, they share similar outlooks with the oracles of doom made against Judah. The deity wishes to punish a named nation and the poetry of the oracle speaks of the military force which will accomplish this and the suffering which will be caused to the population.

The textual engagement with the person of Jeremiah, which occupies a significant amount of space in this book, ends with the story of Jeremiah and the Judahites in Egypt. Following the collection of oracles against other nations there is only one final chapter, chap. 52 and this consists of a third party narration of the fall of Jerusalem. The material is in fact a double of the material concerning the fall of Jerusalem found in the book of 2 Kings. The reader should consider how the account in Jeremiah should be understood in relation to 2 Kings; is either dependent on the other? Does this give any information about the dating of editorial activity in the Jeremiah tradition?

Having read through the book of Jeremiah and noted where individual units of text begin and end, which units are of the same literary type and the dominant vocabulary of each literary style readers can begin to organize their further study of Jeremiah according to the range of reading methodologies made available through the activity of scholars. Much existing scholarship is diachronic which means that it is concerned with the particularity of subsections of the book's contents and with how these subsections relate to one another, set against what can be deduced about events and settings in the later Judahite monarchy and the eventual collapse of Jerusalem. Scholars who are interested less in the composition history of textual units than in the interwoven literary structures of poetry and prose material in the book's final form and those who discuss the rhetorical impact of the book on readers often approach the text synchronically, working with the final form of the canonical book as found in the Masoretic version of the Hebrew Bible and its vernacular translations.

The reading plan set out above assumes the use of an English language text and it is easy for the reader to take the content of the edition used as a fixed basis for textual understanding. However, the original language versions of Jeremiah have been subject not only to translation but also to interpretation, in the process of rendering the material into English. In order to explore other possible translations/interpretations of the biblical material it is good to compare and contrast the approach of different English editions to translating the same passage, as noted above. To that end a short summary of the intentions of major English language editions is provided here. All the major editions of the English version of the Hebrew Bible/Old Testament acknowledge the importance of returning to the original language versions of the text, primarily to the ancient Hebrew and Greek canons.

It is in rendering this material into English that differences of meaning can appear as editors strive to reproduce the original text in English language which will make good sense to their users. One major family of English editions depends on the Authorised Version (KJV) of the Bible made in 1611 under the rule of James I and known also as the King James Bible, an edition which inherited some interpretive strands from earlier English editions made in the second half of the sixteenth century. This edition obviously used the English which was spoken and written in the early seventeenth century and which had become archaic by the twentieth century. In order to render the text more accessible while following the translation guidelines set by the seventeenth-century committee of translators this edition was updated in the twentieth century, first as the Revised Bible (RB) and then as the New English Bible (NEB). The editors of this edition say of their work that their task was to update archaic English while sticking to the text as shaped in the KJV. They note that they have acted as a joint ecumenical committee of editors in order that the edition would be acceptable to many denominations.

The NEB edition was produced from within Church of England circles but a similar project was engaged in by the American Church and took the title of the New International Version (NIV). The editors of this edition note in their preface that they are proud of their system of work which was composed of a three-tiered structure of committees. Translators worked on individual books and submitted their drafts to a higher scrutiny committee which balanced translations of similar words and phrases across all books. A final committee checked the unity of the work performed by the earlier committees. The aim was to provide an edition which followed the KJV tradition and looked back to ancient versions but which had clarity and good literary quality, making it suitable for use in public and private reading, preaching and teaching.

A separate edition which was favoured by the Roman Catholic community took its origins from the French version of the Bible produced by scholars at the Bible school in Jerusalem. The English edition of this was published in the 1960s and known as the Jerusalem Bible (JB). The edition was intended to promote good practice in the Church which kept abreast of the times and deepened theological understanding. It was made for students and for ordinary readers, using today's language and keeping up with the fruits of archaeological and literary research. Once the edition was in use, comments were made that it stuck too much to its French counterpart rather than seeking directly to translate the Hebrew into English. Hence a second edition, known as the New Jerusalem Bible (NJB), was published to answer these criticisms and to continue the task of promoting translations which slotted into contemporary English idiom, making the text more understandable when it was read in public worship contexts.

A further family of texts is found in the RSV and its newer form, the NRSV. The aims of this edition were to provide a standardized English edition which would promote study of the biblical texts. It was an authorised version of the standard American version of 1901, itself a revision of the 1611 edition. The editors wished to bring together the translation insights of the KJV with the fruits of modern scholarship as a basis for the English wording. This edition then gained ecumenical status as the Common English Bible (CEB), meaning that the Roman Catholic community also accepted its worth. In the Catholic editions, however, Deutero-Canonical texts were added in and the preface written by members of the Catholic Biblical Association of Great Britain includes a long explanation of using this extended form of the Old Testament material instead of staying with the shorter version of material found in the Hebrew Rabbinic Bible. This edition was later altered in terms of English usage to make the meaning of the text more accessible to those listening to its being publicly read in a church setting [NRSV].

Finally, many younger readers are familiar with the Good News edition of the English Bible (GNB), since this is often used in schools and colleges. The editors of this material also wished to link with the ancient language texts but wanted their edition to be usable by any reader who could speak English, including non-native English speakers. The aim was to provide a clear articulation of the main contents of the biblical text by the standard of natural, everyday speech. The edition aimed for a 'plain' text which could make use of the natural idiom of the English language and so is less tied to strict parallelism between English wording and original language usages and which emerges from a rolling development of editions which look back to the KJV.

The varied aims of the translators and editors of these editions of the English Bible directly affect the use of English in any given unit of biblical material. When it comes to translating a given page of text the version rendered by one edition can look very different from that produced by another set of editors. Ease of access may lead to simplification of meaning and concepts which underlie whole passages may disappear as each usage is translated on its own terms within its immediate textual context. As an exercise select two poetic passages and two prose passages in Jeremiah and examine the ways in which these subsections are translated in at least three of these editions. What can be gained from this exercise in understanding of the range of possible meanings offered by the Hebrew text?

As an example of this variation in meaning it is possible to examine the call narrative of the prophet in Jeremiah 1 as this is translated by the RSV and the GNB. The RSV stands at the most rigorous end of the spectrum, sticking as much as possible to the original language phrasing, while the GNB works with a free standing approach to translation. Reading both versions of the textual passage under consideration it can be seen that the English of both editions relates to the same original material. Whereas the RSV stays with 'The word of the Lord came…' the GNB changes this to 'The Lord said' making for a simpler and more direct expression. Further on, however, it is harder to see that both English editions have the same original in mind. The task of the prophet is defined in the RSV as being 'consecrated' and 'appointed'; in the GNB the Hebrew is rendered simply by 'selected'.

Both translations convey the sense of a special destiny but the RSV carries the idea of being set apart, put into the divine category by his mission and then in virtue of that status being put in charge of human affairs. By contrast the GNB uses a word which implies a generic process of choosing a messenger, leaving aside the more complex concepts of being made different and thus aligned with an authoritative voice. Carrying out this close examination of parallel English editions with regard to their choice of language enables a reader to go more deeply into the conceptual framework of the original language versions of Jeremiah even without any knowledge of biblical Hebrew or Greek.

As well as engaging in slow and detailed examination of individual passages, it is vitally important that a reader gains a good overall knowledge of the contents of Jeremiah in the English versions, so that there can be awareness of shifts from poetry to prose, the inclusion of self-sufficient units such as the OANs and any major changes in mood within the prophetic text, as in chaps. 30–31 with their message of hope and renewal. When this knowledge of the internal shape of Jeremiah has been gained the reader is ready to examine how the sections of the book of Jeremiah have been interpreted by modern biblical scholarship. Although historical criticism aimed to find the essential meaning of the book, it proved difficult to achieve this goal in ways which would arrive at a conclusive version of the prophet's message. An interest in the literary structure of the book's contents then opened the door to contextual studies which promote meaning as multiple and pluralist, linked to the particular audience of Jeremiah at any given time.

The following chapters provide accounts of these several methods of textual exegesis, returning to subunits of the book, such as prose sermons or prophetic laments, in several individual chapters since the same passages have been interpreted via a number of reading lenses. As with translations into English, the same foundational literary material provokes variant meanings, according to the critical method employed in the process of commentary. These variant meanings are not necessarily exclusive of each other since historical, rhetorical and religious explorations of Jeremiah add depth to our understanding of the book, without inevitably contradicting one another. The character Baruch, for example, can be investigated with regard to possible scribal activity in the late monarchy as well as being subject matter for a reflection as to the ways in which his person is characterized in Jeremiah's story, as helper and follower of a hero figure.

### *Further Reading and References*

The Good News Bible
The Jerusalem Bible/New Jerusalem Bible
The King James Bible
The New English Bible and New International Version
The Revised Standard Version/New Revised Standard Version

All of these English editions of the Bible have multiple printings and can be accessed both in hard copy and online.

Chapter 3

## Historical Criticism and the Study of Jeremiah

Historical-critical enquiry was the first major approach in modern biblical studies to interpreting the book of Jeremiah. The historical project has as its foundation the attribution to author and date found at the start of the book—an historical prophet called Jeremiah and the times of the last kings of Judah. The first task was to examine how far the contents of the book aligned with these attributions of origin in order to arrive at a plain meaning for the text. However, this simple task turned into a more complex project as scholars demonstrated the multiple literary genres which the book contains. It became clear that despite the existence of a named individual attached to prose narratives about his career, together with first person accounts of encounters with the deity, little weight could be placed on these texts as reliable biographical resources. Alongside this realization was the view that the various parts of the book were not the work of a single writer but emerged from a period of textual development—giving rise to the discussion among scholars of the history of composition of the final extant work.

It has already been shown in Chapter 2 that Jeremiah is not systematically written and that different genres sit alongside each other in the final text so the historical task was to identify the oldest material, followed by the individual materials which had been added to that core. It was assumed that the key unit was the words of an historical prophet, which founded the literary tradition. Identification of this material provided a measure by which later additions could be identified in their turn. These various units of text could be understood as originally separate sources which had later been combined. The concept of combination implies editors or redactors whose work added in new material and re-shaped the existing contents of the book.

The approach which scholars developed is, then, one of searching for the history of composition. This work included the separation of embedded units into their former shape, an attempt to date each of these and the consideration of the actual events which led to their production. The lack of surviving examples of written copies of smaller source documents meant that such activity was highly speculative since it is based on reading backwards from a final literary work to presumed earlier versions of the book. It was important to know of any other witnesses to Jeremiah which existed outside the final form of the Masoretic text. The discovery of the Dead Sea Scrolls and gradual translation and publication of the Qumran materials provided evidence of a Jeremiah text from the period of late antiquity. The existence of Jeremiah in other language versions which emerged in the Hellenistic period also provided comparative material. Especially valuable was the form of Jeremiah found in the Septuagint (LXX). Drawing on these several textual resources for Jeremiah studies scholars were able to argue for the viability of producing a reliable account of the development of the literary contents of the book.

In order to develop an understanding of the stages in the production of this historical account of the book of Jeremiah it is useful to begin with the short introduction to Jeremiah written by Robert Carroll (1989/2004). Carroll was himself an expert in the field of Jeremiah studies, producing a full length commentary on this prophetic book in 1986. Carroll's work emerged from within the schools of historical criticism in which he had been trained and his study guide gave thorough attention to the major readings of Jeremiah from the historical perspective, whether literary critical or concerned with the wider socio-political background to which the texts belong.

With regard to history of composition issues, Carroll notes that there is general agreement among historical scholarship that the book of Jeremiah is composed of clear subsections of material which fall into the following categories:

- Chapter 1.1-19 provides a prologue in the form of the call narrative of the prophet
- This is followed by oracles of judgment issued against Judah in chaps. 1–25
- Prose narratives of Jeremiah's messages
- Themes of Judahite renewal as part of a miscellaneous unit of material
- Oracles against other nations
- The story of the fall of Jerusalem and its aftermath
- The last chapter of Jeremiah repeats material also found in 2 Kings 24–25 (Epilogue)

It is this mixture of literary units which provides historical scholarship with its starting point. Scholars have made it clear in identifying these subunits that the book has been gathered together by editors, a viewpoint which is in line with chap. 1.1-3 where an editorial voice summarizes the material as the product of the prophet's activities. So when did this writing/editing take place? What were the concerns of the original communities for whom the book was produced and how might these have shaped its production? These are basic questions of historical criticism.

In addressing such historical enquiries Carroll deals with the significance of the existence of comparative versions of Jeremiah materials. He refers to the fact that we now have two editions of Jeremiah, one based on a Hebrew language tradition and the other on the Greek Septuagint (LXX). The textual contents of each are not exactly the same, even allowing for the impact of translation, as the Greek version is shorter than the Masoretic Hebrew version. Carroll notes that the significance of having recourse to parallel ancient versions of the book is that it illuminates the history of composition through the process of comparing and contrasting actual text, rather than relying on presumed earlier phases of the final edited version of the text of Jeremiah.

Carroll points out, however, that the overall effect on a modern reader of the Jeremiah materials in their collected form is to cause a sense of confusion since the book as a whole does not follow a coherent chronological timeframe nor contextualize separate poetic passages with reference to the dates of events which provided the fulfilment of the disasters referred to in the oracles. It is indeed the fact that the book appears fragmented which has led to the historical search for meaning in relation to the time and manner of its composition. In searching for any point of unity within the text one major possibility is to be found in the prophet himself. As noted above the figure of Jeremiah has quite a high profile in the book, both being described in the third person and being shown as speaking for himself in the first person.

Carroll suggests the importance of exploring the various aspects of Jeremiah's persona as a means of getting into discussion of the book's authority and purpose. He refers to the way in which Jeremiah is presented as a prophet, a divine messenger, in chap. 1, a profile which raises questions about the role of prophets in the world of late monarchy. The editors imply that he is the son of a priest, Hilkiah, so does that mean that the offices of prophet and priest can run together? Jeremiah is an actor on an historical stage, a writer who produces a scroll, who has a secretary, who is a representative of a court faction, a man whose personal pain is synonymous with that of the community as a whole. Yet this wealth of detail is not enough to give us a clear picture of a man's career; Jeremiah remains an ambiguous figure.

Finally, Carroll explores briefly the link between the main book and its final chapter which, in line with a passage from 2 Kings 25, tells the story of the seizure of Jerusalem and its destruction. In terms of history of composition what would have been the point of adding to this prophetic book part of a different work? The destruction of Jerusalem has already been dealt with in Jeremiah chap. 39 so this later chapter goes backwards in time, while giving the event a different emphasis. In this context Carroll offers a close comparison of the contents of the Jeremiah passage as against the contents of the 2 Kings version of events. The Jeremiah version can be seen as expressing the overall theo-politics of the book of Jeremiah, since the religious aspects of the text are continuously aligned with the shifts of power within the region in the period of the seventh–sixth centuries BCE. In particular, contrasting evaluations of the policies of kings Jehoiachin and Zedekiah seem to be at stake in this final chapter when it is compared with chap. 22.

The several chapters of Carroll's short study highlight in these ways the main subsections of historical interest in Jeremiah—the units of material, text composition, the prophet in his background, the unity of theme within the whole book. Specific questions can be asked about the poetic oracles concerning Judah and their links with oracles against other nations. Separate issues arise with regard to the prose material since the tone of Jeremiah's sermons in the early chapters is similar to that of the book of Deuteronomy and the question can validly be asked, does this entail a literary dependency and if so, of what kind? Is Jeremiah to be read as a commentary on the views of Deuteronomy, for instance, or has Jeremiah as a character in the prophetic book been created to match the outline of a 'prophet like Moses', as that concept is defined in Deuteronomy 18? Autobiographical and bio-graphical depictions of the prophet cannot be read simplistically as attempts to document a man's career. They exist as independent literary units which are attuned to the theo-political themes found in the oracular material of the book.

Carroll's introductory book demonstrates the range of questions which historical criticism has produced with regard to Jeremiah. As he notes, we know nothing reliable about the history of the book's composition and its origins: all commentary on these issues remains speculative, producing the-oretical constructions of literary composition. Historical questions remain important but scholarship fails to produce convincing answers to their lines of enquiry. With this perception in place it is possible to turn to the stages of earlier historical research in more detail.

The founder figure of the history of composition research is Bernhard Duhm, whose reading method was that of source criticism, the demonstra-tion of the smaller written documents from which the book as a whole was composed. His commentary divided the book into poetry and prose and argued for a tri-partite order of sources behind the final work (1901). For Duhm the poetic oracles of chaps. 1–25 reflected the work of the histori-cal prophet; this material was collected together by Jeremiah's followers and was attached to a biographical account of Jeremiah made by his scribe Baruch. This combined material provided the earliest layer of Jeremiah tra-ditions, to which were later added supplementary sources of various types, prose materials and OANs, together with editorial comments and expan-sions. Duhm argued for the prime value of a diachronic methodology in interpreting Jeremiah since the book as a whole is a composite work and only by separating out the accretions is it possible to get back to the time of the prophet. It is this first deposit of material which represents the essential message of the book, the words of a man in his own time setting. The book in its final form mostly reflects the views of generations who lived after the time of Jeremiah.

A second major contribution to the history of Jeremiah composition is found in the work of Sigmund Mowinckel (1914). He argued that the book is composed of four individual sources (A, B, C, D) which were joined together, with each being inserted by its own editor. From this material were formed chaps. 1–45; later an appendix of chaps. 46–52 was added together with the final over-arching editorial comment at the start of the book. Mowinckel denoted Source A as the poetry in chaps. 1–25, Source B as historical tales about Jeremiah, Source C as speeches of Jeremiah not found in A or B and having a Deuteronomic style, and Source D as the inverted oracles of chaps. 30–31. In his later thought he described these units not as source documents as such but as contributory materials to a growing Jeremiah tradition.

The main work of scholarship relating to the history of composition subsequent to these early commentaries has been to fine tune and reshape the foundations laid down in these works. One major controversy involves the question of how far it is possible to distinguish the voice of an original prophet from later editing. Is it viable to seek for the message of an historical, independent prophet Jeremiah or should the textual shape of the character Jeremiah be regarded as the formalized mouthpiece for a school of thought which emerged out of exilic experience. In this context particular arguments have arisen over the relationship of Jeremiah and Deuteronomy.

As noted above there is a strong linguistic link between the prose sermons of Jeremiah and parts of the book of Deuteronomy. How should this fact be evaluated? One answer could be that the character Jeremiah has been shaped deliberately to be an expression of 'Torah prophecy'. This would be the work of editors of earlier oracles whose purpose was to link their own, probably exilic, school of thought with a figure from the past, allowing them to claim religious authority in a changed political situation. A second strand of this argument concerns the link between the composition history of Deuteronomy and that of Jeremiah with reference to dating the books. 2 Kings 22 refers to reforms carried out by King Josiah. This scene involves the finding of a book of law in the temple archives which was then made into the foundation of Josianic reform. Scholarship suggested that this book could have been either Deuteronomy or proto-Deuteronomy; since Jeremiah's sermons echo themes from Deuteronomy it could have been part of the writing carried out by a particular faction in the royal court, or it could have been aligned with a Deuteronomic viewpoint after the collapse of the monarchy and at the time of the return from exile in Babylonia.

Since it is impossible to define accurately the dates of the re-shaping of material within Jeremiah tradition William McKane suggests it is best to argue simply for a rolling expansion of material within the literary tradition of Jeremiah (1986). History of composition research has shown that the breaking of the text into discrete units, which may come from different times and editors, is valid but this does not mean that readers can identify the author and date of these passages. Ancient writers were less concerned with promoting their personal identity than with their work being attributed to heroic figures from tradition, thus demonstrating the continued relevance of older teaching in new social and political contexts.

The matter of defining the final level of authorship is equally complex. Even if it is agreed that a Deuteronomic approach has shaped the final form of chaps. 1–25, and that this links the material to exilic times, the question arises as to where among the distribution of Judahites outside the land did the exilic editor live and work. The prose narratives describing Jeremiah's last activities link the prophet to dispersed communities both in Egypt and Babylon. But it is also possible that the final editing happened after the restoration of a temple-focused theocratic province, Yehud, within the Persian Empire. In this case, the final layer of text production represents the claims of that generation to authenticate their authority in Jerusalem. The book of Jeremiah could thus bear traces of several different ideologies which emerged in Judah between the late monarchy and the Persianled restoration.

These attempts to date the stages of production of Jeremiah can be set alongside the parallel historical enquiry which turns on the use of comparative material existing in different language versions of the book. This form of exploration focuses mainly on Hebrew and Greek versions of Jeremiah. The Rabbinic Bible takes as its standard the Masoretic Hebrew versions of the Hebrew Scriptures. This witness to the text of Jeremiah links with the production of the canonical Hebrew Bible, especially with the work of the Jewish Masoretic scholars of the tenth-eleventh centuries CE. A second version of the material is found in the Greek LXX, a version which tradition suggests was made deliberately to translate inherited sacred works for Jewish communities which were Greek-speaking, such as in the city of Alexandria. Although there is some doubt as to the veracity of the details of this story, as told in the *Letter to Aristeas*, the LXX became a major witness to Jewish tradition in the Hellenistic world. By comparison of the two versions it can be seen that the LXX presents a shorter version of the book of Jeremiah and the Masoretic text (MT) a longer version. This difference opens up speculation concerning the complexity of the historical transmission of the prophetic book.

The discovery of fragments of Hebrew Jeremiah at Qumran which are parallel with the contents of the Septuagint version suggest that there may have been an earlier Hebrew manuscript tradition which has undergone change and development in transmission. The LXX version has fewer repetitions of words and phrases than the MT and the OANs follow chaps. 1–25. The MT expands the use of the term for prophet '*ha nabi*' and puts the OANs later in the work and it may be to this later stage of compilation that the prose Deuteronomic elements belong. These findings reinforce the view that the current book of Jeremiah is the result of a long process of reshaping but they do not directly tell us anything about the details of changes in text shape, the dates at which these shifts occurred, or the intentions of the redactors and the nature of their audiences.

One detailed study of the possible interlinks between Hebrew and Greek versions of the text of Jeremiah is found in the work of Andrew Shead (2002). He examines Jeremiah 32 in its MT and LXX forms, breaking the chapter into sections: vv. 1-15, 16-25, 26-35, 36-44. His aim is to draw out from the versions the original format of the material in the chapter and to define the line of development from early M (Hebrew) and G (Greek) to MT and LXX respectively. After close examination of the Hebrew and Greek final versions of the text of Jeremiah and their use of language, Stead admits that this aim is not capable of success while working only within the method of literary dependency which seeks to show how a later version of a text depends on the form of an earlier available version of content which is common to both textual versions. He suggests that it would be necessary to invoke redactional theory and its reading lens in order to give a fuller account of textual development. Shead's work highlights both the aspirations of historical criticism to identify the exact stages of compositional change in the Jeremiah materials and the difficulties of arriving at definitive conclusions about dating significant moments in this process.

Whatever viewpoint is taken regarding the historical composition of Jeremiah, it is clear that the biblical text deals not simply with religious belief but with the political events of the region in which action is set. This reality gives rise to a different form of historical enquiry, one which aligns with archaeology. The book of Jeremiah assumes a time setting of monarchy, at the stage of Judahite history when the kingdom was threatened by foreign powers—the enemy from the north. The prose narratives identify some of these opponents as rulers of ancient Babylon, such as King Nebuchadrezzar (chap. 39). Can this style of literary reference be endorsed from a different angle? Archaeologists of the ancient Near East have sought out the witness to such ancient cultures in the sands of Mesopotamia, in tells which represent the buried remains of ancient cities. Excavations of ancient imperial sites such as the royal palaces of Nineveh, Nimrud and Babylon have provided a balance to the biblical record. Friezes on the palace walls depict the great triumphs of the rulers; one of these, for instance, deals with the campaigns of the Assyrians in Judah, showing in detail the capture of the city of Lachish, a city site in Judah.

Archaeological research has revealed a political reality similar to that found in the setting of Jeremiah, a period which saw the rise of a northern superpower in Mesopotamia—first neo-Assyria, then Babylon. These societies were imperialistic in intent and extended their control of territory southwards, ultimately destroying Jerusalem. After a period of political vacuum in the narrow strip of land which links Egypt in the south with Mesopotamia in the north, an event which allowed small indigenous kingdoms to develop, the more usual power balance of domination by either Egypt or Mesopotamia re-asserted itself. That this is the context for much of Jeremiah can be seen not only in poetic threats of an enemy from the north but also in the prose narratives, where the prophetic voice argues against trusting in an alliance with Egypt against Babylonian supremacy. The overall historical connections of the book of Jeremiah to the wider ancient Near East can thus be validated. But that does not mean that details of events can be firmly set out. The Lachish frieze, for example, proves that Judah and Jerusalem were threatened by invading forces but there is no parallel account in the book of Jeremiah to the visual narrative of the frieze. The reader becomes aware that Jeremiah makes use of general contexts but is not in itself a documentary history of political details.

The focus of the book of Jeremiah is rather one of theo-politics, as Carroll noted. The overall narrative structure of Jeremiah weaves together historical regional politics with the cult of a particular God who is viewed as the only valid patron deity for the Judahite kingdom. The main characters of the book are kings, priests, prophets and court officials, providing a set of characters which defines the city of Jerusalem as the central sanctuary of YHWH as well as the focal point for royal power. Characters, plot and setting in Jeremiah 1–45 interact to promote the topic of theo-politics in which the critical question of regime survival is linked to proper forms of public cult.

This is found, for example, in the prose sermons, as in chap. 7, where from a site at the temple gate the prophet critiques a complacent reliance on divine support on the part of the worshippers who enter the temple. In the prose narratives it becomes clear that the royal household contains different political factions, either siding with the Babylonian overlords or advocating rebellion against them. The critical issue is which side is the deity on in this dispute. The prophet Jeremiah operates both as an organ of divine judgment against the elite culture as a whole for its service of a number of deities and as the voice of the party of peace with the Babylonians.

A clear example of the mixing of religious and political themes is found in Jer. 11.1-17 where the prophet is urged by God to speak to the people of

Jerusalem and Judah about necessary loyalty to the Covenant made by the deity with the Israelites as they left Egypt. The LORD notes that the people have abandoned that loyalty by returning to idolatry and polytheistic worship. As a result of this breach of covenant duties a great disaster will be brought down on the people. Symbolically, it will be as though a great storm descends on the land burning up all the trees and bringing ruin. In this passage of the prose sermons, the interweaving of religion and politics in the ideology of covenant relationship expresses the first part of the task given to Jeremiah in chap. 1, that of tearing down.

But the negative aspect of covenantal theology is balanced by references to a future restoration of the covenant—understood as a form of 'treaty' between God and the people. Although most of the material in chaps. 1–45 is concerned with divine cursing, chaps. 30–31 stand out as a counterbalance to doom. They reflect on the future beyond the end of society as it has been, promising a restoration of land ownership, a great agricultural prosperity and a new alliance between God and people. This section of text exemplifies the second part of Jeremiah's role as set out in chap. 1, which is to build up. Whether society declines or flourishes, however, is depicted as entirely dependent on the favour of a patron deity, under the theme of cursing and blessing. Politics is defined by divine authority.

Hence Jeremiah is primarily a text which promotes the worship of one deity, viewing ownership of land as a gift from the God who owns it. Other nations may claim supremacy as a result of having superior military force but Jeremiah argues for a geopolitics in which those great nations are not greater than the God of Israel, since the invader is permitted to cause difficulties as a form of punishment and awakening directed towards a chosen society. As the book fleshes out its religious language of sin and punishment, of true and false religion, it can be seen that political affairs are always close to the surface. The Judahite kings are caught between factions for war and for peace. Part of the endorsement of Jeremiah's religious viewpoint comes from his profile as spokesman for the peace faction; hence both religious and secular matters are managed in the book through the profiling of the prophet himself.

This textual reality focuses historical enquiry on history of composition matters. If Jeremiah is viewed as an historical personage, one who analyses news of regional military deployments and assesses the likelihood of defeat, the text carries the pathos of a doomed culture which envisages its own end. If Jeremiah is seen as a character whose profile expresses the views of those who later took control of Judah, who justify their claim to power by creating a character whose mission was to bring down the past government on the grounds of religious unworthiness, the reader is faced with a form of political propaganda. Both historical contexts can be justified given the content of history of composition scholarship.

Since the character Jeremiah holds together the material found in chaps. 1–45 of the book, and his mantle is cast over the Oracles against the Nations also, scholars have given serious thought to the task of retrieving the historical prophet from the text. However, the characterization of Jeremiah works very well when evaluated more as a literary tool to dramatize the message of the book than as an expression of historical reality. Jeremiah 1, for example, can be interpreted as the initiation of this focus with its use of first person speech and with the concept of divine ownership of Jeremiah's destiny, planned out for him before his birth. A further device to forefront Jeremiah comes in Jeremiah 7, where the anonymous storyteller describes the scene at the Temple gates and records the very words of the prophet. The return to first-person speech in Jeremiah 11 and following, as Jeremiah laments the effect of his ministry on his interior state, heightens the pathos of the prophet's profile.

Historical enquiry into the possible origins of the book of Jeremiah interests itself also in one of the other actors in the text. In the prose narratives, Jeremiah is shown to have one particular companion, his scribe Baruch. This reference to a scribal companion provides the access point for historical research into the possibility that sections of this material were composed by Baruch, from his memoirs of the time. It is then possible to suggest that chaps. 1–24, Jeremiah's poetic oracles, were preserved by this same figure and that this material was handed on to new generations once the events envisaged in the material took place. It is important to remember here that the figure of Baruch, like that of Jeremiah, functions as a symbolic figure within the text-world. Baruch, as identified in the book of Jeremiah, could be the way in which later editors mark their own interests in the Jeremiah tradition. Baruch could be a figure from the late monarchy but could also be the character worked out by a post-exilic redactor keen to show continuity between his own regime and the memories of past elites.

A further point of concern with regard to prophets and scribes is how named figures fit into the wider role of prophecy in the local culture of the ancient Near East. Historical criticism seeks to access the live context of prophetic activity which underlies the written material. Jeremiah is depicted as a priest's son and as a royal official, a prophet, one who is consulted with regard to the proper policy which kings should adopt. To that extent he is part of the elite class, situated at the centre of power; yet he is also shown as a loner, isolated from his fellow citizens by his prophetic mission, which is viewed less as a civic function and more as an inspired proclamation of truth. Across the writings collectively labelled *nebiim* in the Hebrew Bible certain stereotypical behaviour for prophets emerges. Particularly relevant here are the works which contain pre-exilic scenes and teaching. The paradigm of the prophet found in these materials, like that of Jeremiah, reflects the paradoxical role of the prophet as insider/outsider of the central ruling classes, indicating that prophets might be set apart from, and in opposition to, temple officials and kings. But is this an historical fact or a literary device used to endorse religio-political teaching, linking the deity with Babylonian supremacy?

One aspect of the debate concerning the roles of prophets in ancient Judah is the fact that the prophet who forms the major character in each of these books is portrayed as a lone individual whose voice provides unique commentary on events of the time. In the case of the monarchic period in Judah, however, two men are depicted as operating at royal courts in the monarchic period and with a parallel message of judgment—Jeremiah and Isaiah. Although they are not exact contemporaries, the work of each man is not known to the other, it seems, since the book of Jeremiah does not mention a similar mission by Isaiah, and vice versa. Surely, if the historical settings are realistic, these two prophets of judgment could be expected to have knowledge of parallel prophetic ministry in Judah. It is, therefore, possible to suggest that the depiction of the prophet as a single lone individual acting differently from other courtiers such as priests and fellow prophets is a literary phenomenon and not necessarily historically accurate.

Jeremiah 28, for example, indicates that more than one official at court could be called a prophet, since it shows Hananiah uttering an oracle and performing ritual symbolic action related to that message in a parallel manner to that of Jeremiah, thus narrating a contest between two prophets. Only one of the two, however, is revealed as a prophet of truth. The chapter profiles Jeremiah as performing the same actions but in order to promote the opposite advice to the king from that of Hananiah. The topic of true and false prophecy is one which assumes that a number of figures exist who are known as prophets and who perform duties within the royal household as advisors and councillors. Yet the link between secular politics and theological message is in fact undermined by the way in which written prophecy emphasizes that these figures come to their role as a result of divine intervention—as shown in Jeremiah 1.

This chapter has identified a number of particular debates within the broad range of historical enquiry concerning the book of Jeremiah. The central area of enquiry has been the history of the composition of the final form of the book. This strand of research had its foundations laid in the work of Duhm and Mowinckel but is still live insofar as no compelling answers have, as yet, been provided to the dating of sections of the book or to their authorship. Further resources for the debate have been provided by investigation of comparative versions of Jeremiah but these also produce no conclusive answer to issues of authorship, date and provenance. Finally, enquiry has branched out into wider matters of political and cultural history of the ancient Near East. In a number of issues, these investigations have provided relevant settings for the specific debates concerning Jeremiah as prophet and the rise of regional superpowers and their impact on Judah but they, too, have not answered the specific historical queries about the man and his ministry, his followers and his editors. The floor remains open on these matters.

## *Further Reading and References*

Carroll, R.
    1986    *Jeremiah: A Commentary* (London: SCM Press).
    1989    *Jeremiah* (Sheffield: JSOT Press [repr. London: T. & T. Clark, 2004]).
Duhm, B.
    1901    *Das Buch Jeremia* (Tübingen: Mohr).
Garcia Martinez, F., and W. Watson (eds.)
    1996    *The Dead Sea Scrolls Translated: The Qumran Texts in English* (Leiden: Brill).
McKane, W.
    1986    *A Critical and Exegetical Commentary on Jeremiah* (Edinburgh: T. & T. Clark).
Mitchell, T.
    2004    *The Bible in the British Museum: Interpreting the Evidence* (London: British Museum). See also the website, www.thebritishmuseum.ac.uk (Western Asian section).
Mowinckel, S.
    1914    *Zur Komposition des Buches Jeremia* (Oslo: Jacob Dybwad).
Shead, A.
    2002    *The Open Book and the Sealed Book: Jeremiah 32 in its Hebrew and Greek Recensions* (Edinburgh: T. & T. Clark).

*The Letter of Aristeas* (various sources including the following one)

Charlesworth, J. (ed.)
    1988    *The Pseudepigrapha of the Old Testament*, vol. 2 (New York: Doubleday).

Chapter 4

THE CONTINUING ROLE OF HISTORICAL CRITICAL ENQUIRY

The previous chapter explored the fundamental issues involved in the historical-critical approach to studying the book of Jeremiah. It was shown that this field of research is composed of a number of approaches within the overarching designation of the history of composition. One major investigation focuses on the textual contents of Jeremiah and seeks to find the smaller older units of material now combined into a single work in order to trace the history of composition. Related to this are two further lines of exploration. One approach is to locate the editors who redacted the work into its final shape. In the case of Jeremiah this has involved comparative research between the prophetic book and other canonical texts which have been labelled by scholars as Deuteronomic in style, linked with the vocabulary and argument of the book of Deuteronomy. A second engages scholars in the comparison of the Hebrew version of Jeremiah with that of the ancient Greek text of the book. A further historical viewpoint moves outside biblical text to consider the social organizations, political events and cultural norms of Judah and its ancient Near Eastern setting which formed the context in which biblical material emerged. In Jeremiah studies, all these strands are linked with issues about the historicity of the account given in the text of the life and work of the individual prophet.

This second chapter on historical criticism starts from the introduction to the field of study provided in the previous chapter and builds on those foundations in terms of the extensions to the strands of compositional enquiry made by more recent scholarship in this area. Broadly speaking, the central focus remains the attempt to trace the origins of the Jeremiah material and to define the mode and meaning of the earliest layers in the tradition. Hence the methodological foundations set by Duhm and Mowinckel remain the point of departure for historical critics, even though later scholarship has nuanced the views of these 'classic' theories of the formation of the book of Jeremiah.

The continuity of the historical-critical approach beyond the initial phase of research into the book of Jeremiah in modern times is indicated by the contents of a recent book of essays edited by John Goldingay (2007). In terms of the study of history of composition, for example, the volume includes papers that propose settings for Jeremiah from late monarchical times to the Persian period. Although Goldingay himself does not provide an editorial section which undertakes to flesh out the details of developing methods in Jeremiah studies, the essay by Lawrence Boadt on the issue of whether Jeremiah and Ezekiel contain a common view of the exile includes material which provides a summary of the history of thought with regard to the figure of Jeremiah. This essay also offers a useful summary of the developments in historical criticism of the book of Jeremiah.

Boadt notes that the basis for all later studies remains that of the views of Duhm and Mowinckel but, looking back across some decades of scholarship, it is clear that their conclusions with regard to author, date and audience of the book have been challenged by later readings of the history of composition. Theorists who found three individual sources embedded in the final text have been robustly critiqued; the view that the voice of the original prophet can be found in the first 20 chapters of poetic oracles no longer gains an easy acceptance. Meanwhile, the separation of prose narratives from prose sermons has been negatively valued since the language of both of these units shows similar tendencies. It is clear from Boadt's summary that scholars continue to be concerned with the search for the historical prophet and that there is agreement with the argument that the contents of Jeremiah show signs of a gradual build-up of passages which add to and interpret older material for fresh audiences, through into the context of post-exilic Judah. It is also accepted that the clear definitions between layers of the tradition which earlier scholars proposed no longer carry weight, as against the view that the process of addition was gradual and interwove new insights with existing text.

Outside the immediate field of historical dating of units of material there have been developments in other aspects of the field of historical investigation. Insights into changes in these other fields are provided by the contents of the Goldingay volume. Contributions cover a number of the sub-fields set out in the previous chapter—from textual composition, to the figure of the prophet, to wider socio-cultural topics. These essays include possible dating of the material based on comparative exploration of the witnesses to the Jeremiah tradition, comparative accounts of Jeremiah in the context of other Hebrew Bible works, reflections on the profile of Jeremiah himself, on the work of editors and on the wider study of ancient Near Eastern culture. In addition, some new perspectives on the function of literature, such as that provided by ideological criticism, are applied to historical research.

There have, for example, been refinements with regard to the growth of the Jeremiah tradition as witnessed to by manuscript families, as indicated in debates concerning the nature of the relationship of the shorter LXX version to the longer MT version of Jeremiah. Scholars have noted that Deuteronomic language is used in the shared materials of the Greek and Hebrew versions rather than in the extra material found in the longer MT; hence it is possible to suggest that such language will have been part of the earliest witnesses to the Jeremiah tradition. In his essay, Roy Wells develops an argument regarding the significance of the LXX material as an indicator of the earlier Hebrew text of Jeremiah, pointing to fragments of Hebrew text found in the discoveries in the Judean desert as proof of this, since they seem to be the prototypes of the Greek version. From this basis he explores the construction of Jeremiah 28 positing two layers of writing within the Hananiah scene—an original account of a symbolic action of Jeremiah which has been qualified by the later introduction of a time element to the material. Taken together, these passages address the theme of true and false prophets and their role as sent by the deity or not—a theme which can be viewed as a significant shaper of meaning in this passage.

Within the boundaries of historical approaches to the origins of the book of Jeremiah a key issue remains that of the place of the figure of the individual prophet. Boadt discusses scholarly views on the dating of Jeremiah's call, noting that chap. 1 of the book suggests a date of 627 BCE whereas Holladay and others have argued for a date of 622 or 609 BCE, connecting the prophetic call with the trigger of Josiah's death. The earlier date allows for the presence of Deuteronomic thought in Jeremiah through the possible connection between the prophetic language and the account of the finding of a law book in Josiah's time, reported in 2 Kings 22. Boadt notes that scholarship which continues to support the later date would have more difficulty in explaining how the prophet was connected with the reforms of King Josiah's reign recorded in 2 Kings.

The profile of the prophet's life is highlighted more in Jeremiah than in the other major prophetic books and this has led to debates about the possibility of reading the text as providing raw data for Jeremiah's career. Boadt notes that the function of Jeremiah as a Deuteronomic preacher does not adequately cover his overall image within the book and argues that this is better described as the paradigm of a Torah prophet, like Moses. Jeremiah 26.16-24 may suggest that Jeremiah is to be understood as one figure within a line of oracular messengers whose message did not find an easy reception at court. It is not only Jeremiah whose career receives scholarly attention; Baruch is a second figure whose life is depicted in the book of Jeremiah and whose role in history and as a literary figure can validly be investigated.

While most of the essays explore an historical line of textual development which leads back towards the monarchical era, that by John Hill picks up the idea that the timespan of composition extended into the Second Temple period. One argument in support of this perspective is the fact that the joint LXX and MT material view Babylon as an actual historical force, whereas the longer MT unit views the city as an archetypal symbol of a hostile state. Hill suggests that the closure of the MT version of Jeremiah may not have been until the fourth/third centuries BCE. Jeremiah 33.14-26 gives details of a Davidic ruler who will emerge to lead the state but this is connected with divine promises rather than actual events. The focus in the book on that promise, allied with the centrality of Levitical priesthood and the restoration of worship, could provide a writing context of the Persian period, even though the format is not the same as that found in Second Temple works such as the book of Zechariah.

A number of papers discuss aspects of Jeremiah in relation to broad cultural settings in antiquity, such as Lundberg's comparison of Jer. 10.1-16 with Mesopotamian incantation rituals and Michael Moore's comparison of the prophet's laments with 1QH. Leo Perdue focuses on the role of Baruch as a Deuteronomic sage and contextualizes the literary figure of Baruch-as-scribe with material drawn more widely from portrayals of sages and scribes in the Babylonian and Persian periods. William Domeris turns to the metaphoric use of agricultural images in Jeremiah, trying to flesh out their message in connection with the agricultural society of monarchic times, discussing the balance between peasantry and urbanization, using the imagery of land as wasted and as fertile as an example of textual usage which links theo-politics with lived experience. These treatments take an historical approach to interpretation of Jeremiah, not in terms of the history of composition but more from a social approach to the function of literature and the interaction between metaphors and the cultural settings of urban and rural life in the ancient Near East.

Close reading of the literary construction of text can lead to a focus on the passage's ideology, on how it is shaped towards emphasizing one particular attitude to politics or society, producing the reading methodology of ideological criticism. This is a line of enquiry which emerged in recent times as part of modern literary criticism and which has then been applied in interpretation of biblical literature. This method concerns itself with the rhetoric of persuasion which writers employ in text production and which can be harnessed in support of political authority. Nancy Lee's essay on the topic of singers of lament presses beyond literary forms to the ideologies which such forms construct.

In this approach, interpretation consists not simply of an examination of the internal poetics of a piece of literature but moves from that examination to evaluate the message which is thereby produced. Texts function socio-rhetorically, Lee argues, in the ancient world as in modern times. Ideological criticism leads Goldingay to consider the 'superpower' imagery of the book of Jeremiah and the use of imperialist language to support Jeremiah's message, namely that Judah is intended by transcendent power to be a vassal state of the Babylonians. However, this does not make imperial claims that sovereign states operate under no authority but their own paramount. Instead, the book of Jeremiah both uses imperial language and at the same time refutes it, as the final denunciation of Babylon's hold on politics in the OANs demonstrates.

Goldingay's volume, with its range of historical topics, shows that questions of composition history and the possible intertextual cross-references between Jeremiah and other biblical works have remained staple matters for scholarly research up till the present day. Although, as Boadt points out, there have been revisions of the work of the founders of historical research in Jeremiah studies in modern times, scholars continue to search for greater precision concerning author, date and context for the composition and editing of units of prophetic material. At the same time, fresh methodological approaches to exegesis of biblical material, such as the study of social-linguistic terms of reference and ideological criticism, have emerged from the field of modern literary and cultural criticism. In some cases scholars have combined insights drawn from these contemporary interests with historical concerns connected to an underlying orientation to the fabric of cultures in antiquity.

One topic which has remained central to historical scholarship is the question of Deuteronomic editing within Jeremiah. A number of researchers have written on this aspect of composition history, with particular concern for the identification of Deuteronomic language and beliefs within the book. This approach both aligns Jeremiah with the thought world of Deuteronomy and highlights the specific usage of parallel perspectives in the prophetic work. Mark Leuchter (2005) explores the use of the term '*maqom*' [place] in the prose sermons, arguing that Jer. 7.1-15 alters the function of the term, normally attributed to the Jerusalem temple, by employing Deuteronomistic scribal methods similar to the style of those scribes who used the term for Josianic purposes. In his 2008 monograph on this topic he argues for reading Jeremiah 26–45 as an independent unit shaped by Deuteronomic scribes who were in conflict with Zadokite claims to power in the exilic context. By inserting their material within a book which contained the work of an earlier and respected prophetic tradition they sought to gain control socially. Matthijs de Jong (2011) took up the topic of true and false prophecy by arguing that Jeremiah uses Deut. 18.15-22, rules for judging prophets, and making it problematic by positing the view that the prophet's role is not to be a foreseer but a source of moral guidance.

By contrast with such tightly focused textual comparisons, parallelism between the two biblical works can be harnessed to the whole task of compositional exploration. Michael Williams (1993), for instance, tackles the entire paradigm of documentary composition from its origins with the work of Duhm and Mowinckel, using their frameworks of source theory with reference to the prose sermons to explore whether Mowinckel's account of sources B and C [referred to above] is to be nuanced with regard to Deuteronomic theology. Williams' article exemplifies the significance of the work of early scholarship within Jeremiah studies and provides a further layer in the use of source theory as a tool for examining the book's discrete sections.

There have been contributions also to the field of dating passages from Jeremiah via reading back from a passage's content to the possible time and place of the origins of that material. Simon Chavel (1997) investigates how the emancipatory text of Jer. 34.8-14 is linked textually with the event in which king Zedekiah's group emancipated all Hebrew slaves while Jerusalem was besieged. He reads this passage in two parts, treating Zedekiah's action as reflective of actual events which are based on a report of historical events which took place in a distant past (vv. 12-14). Chavel concludes that the linking of these two events allowed the author of chap. 34 the opportunity to renew previous attitudes to Judean 'Hebrew' slavery. In this reading strategy, the biblical text is treated as providing historical evidence for the past in its creation of a chain of chronological events. Chavel's exegesis implies that a literary record can become the basis for renewed historical activity which itself turns into a literary deposit, thus producing a report on how one social structure developed over time—in this case slavery.

The work of Carolyn Sharp (2000) provides a second example of this style of exegesis. She examines possible intertexts between the call of Jeremiah as prophet and the nature of diaspora politics. She notes that Jeremiah's role as prophet to the nations is problematic given the biblical account of his career and argues that scholarship has adjusted this profile to focus on Jeremiah's work in Israel. She suggests viewing the prophet's function as described in chap. 1 in the light of chaps. 25.9-38, 27.1-11 and 2.8 in order to demonstrate that Jer. 1.5 was subject to development in two ways, one of which reflected the political interests of court officials and others deported to Babylon, and a second strand attached to the editorial group based in Palestine who resisted the textual interpretation of the returnees from exile.

Sharp notes that the first passage in the list announces the exile but in v. 12 states that after 70 years this will be reversed, with the foreign nations being punished for their aggressive stance. The second passage refers to the same disaster but stresses servitude to Babylon as a continuous reality, whereas the third passage has the message of breaking Babylon's supremacy. This article, like that of Chavel, combines focused textual study with a wider appeal to the historical foundations of textual messages in order to explore the cultural setting from which a literary passage emerges and how it is shaped by performing the role of communicating meaning within its social context.

Intertextual exegesis has also had a wider part to play in the development of historical criticism of the book of Jeremiah as, for example, with the possible links between ancient versions of the book in terms of the dating of additions to the literary tradition. With regard to such textual witnesses to Jeremiah, James Watts (1992) examined the possible redactional history of the OANs in Jeremiah, based on comparative study of the MT and LXX versions of this material and their prototypes. Watts' study exemplifies also the potential value of investigating further the complexity of the relationship between language versions within antiquity, a research project which was one of the foundations of historical criticism. The examination of the contents of the oracles against nations other than Judah offers a specific example of this exegetical method.

This material forms a subsection of its own with the style of cursing oracles found in chaps. 1-25 addressed to Judah now applied to a number of ancient Near Eastern states. This material has an editorial introduction which states Jeremiah's task to be a prophet to the nations, implying that what follows is part of his unique role. This is in keeping with the book of Jeremiah's presentation of the main character as a man alone, destined for a special mission. Yet the OANs are found in other written books of prophecy, such as Isaiah and Ezekiel, and their contents are very similar across these individual renderings.

In Jeremiah they provide a section of text which is situated in the later part of the book, whereas in the other two major works of prophecy they are in the middle. Equally, the LXX version of Jeremiah places this material in the middle of the book. It appears that the OANs were recognized as independent material within the time of the writers and editors of the Jeremiah tradition and were deliberately inserted. This textual reality engages the reader in the complexity of evaluating the whole presentation of Jeremiah as having an individual role in society and as operating in a singular manner at roughly the same period as Isaiah. It also sheds a particular light on the idea that much of the material in Jeremiah can be attributed to a single speaker of oracles, as Holladay sought to argue.

As well as addressing relationships between textual witnesses as a form of intertextuality, this exegetical method can also be used to examine the possible overlaps between canonical prophetic books. In this category can be found Benjamin Sommer's article (1999) linking the redactional history of Jeremiah with the contents of the book of Isaiah, seeing references to Jeremiah in Isaiah chaps. 40–66 and 34–35. Jeremiah's oracles in the first section of the book carry images of land withering and of social collapse and Sommer notes that Isaiah 34–35 also uses apocalyptic language. In a similar manner, Jeremiah's mood shifts to joyful renewal in Jeremiah 30–31, a move parallel with the content and message of Isaiah 40–66. Because these sections of biblical text can be identified as literary forms in their own right, it appears that there is a consistent use of specific blocks of material in both prophetic books. Sommer argues that his intertextual study provides evidence to support source-critical hypotheses regarding the book of Jeremiah.

Also in intertextual perspective, Holladay (2001) explored the possible links between Jeremiah and Ezekiel, asking whether Ezekiel could have

known Jeremiah personally. This piece of research moves behind existing text to the wider question raised in the previous chapter as to the historical authenticity of the paradigm of the lone prophet. Holladay argues
his viewpoint with reference to the date of Jer. 15.15-18, set against the
dating of Ezekiel's work. Jeremiah 15.16, for instance, speaks of eating
the words of God and Ezekiel 1–3 contains the image of the prophet told
to eat a scroll which appears before him. Meanwhile, Jerry Gladon's article (2001) approaches the issue of links between Deuteronomy and Jeremiah from an intertextual angle in which the book of Jeremiah is viewed as
a conscious commentary on the earlier book. Gladon studied Jer. 17.19-27
as a case of re-writing the Sinaitic code. In this intertextual case study, he
puts the text of Deuteronomy side by side with the fresh halakhic expan-
sions drawn from prophetic experience. Deuteronomy's account of the laws
of the sabbath day are repeated in Jeremiah 17 with the comment that they
are suitable formulas for the Judah of Jeremiah's experience, especially as
the prophet expresses this view while standing at the temple gates (v. 19).

So far in this chapter, it has been shown how essential ideas about the
original shape of the book of Jeremiah have provided methodologies for
later historical critical scholarship. Many short papers have developed lines
of interpretation which nuance major interpretive viewpoints by reference to
close textual analysis of small, coherent sections of the book. In some cases,
the historical approach is adopted without question, as with Chavel's paper
on Hebrew slavery. In other examples given here, the historical approach
works by treating texts as historical 'remains' which can consciously be
placed side by side as a means of pressing forward knowledge of the history
of composition; all intertextual projects referred to above fit into this category. These forms of textual research mostly employ techniques set out in
the twentieth century but Goldingay's volume demonstrates how newer literary critical theory can also be applied to the book of Jeremiah, in order to
put forward suggestions about authorial intention or audience reception of
the material. Goldingay's own article on ideological criticism and imperial
concepts fits into this category.

The later phases of historical criticism, then, mix older styles of exegesis with newer approaches. Questions of historical context and order of
composition continue to be of interest to scholars but recent collections of
essays on this book include, alongside historical documentary treatments,
approaches from other perspectives. The volume edited by Hans Barstad
and Reinhard Kratz (2009) reflects this state of affairs in Jeremiah studies.
On the one hand, Graeme Auld's paper continues the questioning of a possible Deuteronomistic layer of editing in Jeremiah by pointing out the over-
lap between 1 Sam. 3.11 (disaster is brought on the sons of Eli), 2 Kgs 21.12
(disaster will come down on Jerusalem) and Jer. 19.3, which deals with the
fate of Jerusalem.

Barstad's own paper connects textual motifs with the field of cultural study since it considers the issue of divine revelation in Jeremiah, linking some examples of this event with typical biblical modes such as dreams and formal consultations of the deity, set within an ancient Near Eastern context. From this setting, out of the problem, Barstad moves on to consider in what ways Jeremiah might stand out as original, rather than manifest a stereotype of prophetic activity. He finds his answer in the argument that the many first person reports mark the prophetic profile in a unique way. Here Barstad moves between the lone prophet profile given inside Jeremiah and the comparative cultural environment of divination, in order to endorse the biblical view of Jeremiah as a prophet set against other court officials.

On the other hand, Lester Grabbe's essay uses modern social anthropology to explore Jeremiah's profile, setting his biblical persona alongside evidence from the modern Nuer culture, evidence which shows how spirit mediums can support guerrilla movements which criticize the existing government, using the icon of a central scribal figure. From this modern socio-cultural application Grabbe also endorses the biblical presentation of Jeremiah as critic of royal policy and opponent of other factions in the royal court. In both cases the use of socio-cultural examples explores and makes sense of the possible historical authenticity of the characterization of Jeremiah the prophet.

Alongside these historical-cultural concerns, the papers in Barstad's volume demonstrate an interest in the literary aspects of Jeremiah. Whereas Elizabeth Hayes uses the modern linguistic tool of cognitive linguistics to examine the textual use of symbolic language in prophetic vision, Christoph Bultmann applies a more ancient concept of epigrammatist to the artistic construction of language in Jeremiah. Joachim Schaper uses a literary theme to consider the historical development of Israelite religion, seeing in the scene of the prophet dictating to a scribe imaged in Jeremiah 36 a new event in ancient religious traditions; here the text is conserved in a conscious effort to provide a basis for oral recitation.

A self-aware examination of the viability of creating such reading methods from a basis of taking a plain reading of text and applying modern methods of interpretation is provided by two papers in the Barstad volume. The tension between cultural and literary approaches is openly addressed by Martti Nissinen, in his examination of the debate between Carroll and Thomas Overholt as to whether prophecy is a social or a literary phenomenon. Meanwhile, Stuart Weeks brings the ambiguous nature of prophecy to the forefront in his article about Jeremiah as a prophetic book. What is prophecy, he asks, since a book is not exactly an act of prophecy in itself. His paper engages the student of biblical text with the inevitable gap between what happens and how happenings are written about after the event. This comes back to the debate between Carroll and Overholt as to whether prophecy is primarily an event, which is later described, or primarily a piece of literature which in some way takes an event as its origin.

Other contributors to the Barstad volume assume a general link between text and reality and use this as a basis to enquire into the nature of theology in dialogue with politics. In this approach, the dynamic of historical activity is taken as a foundation for the drawing out of religious ideas, as in David Reimer's paper on the political theology of Jeremiah and Rannfrid Thelle's study of the use of the name Babylon in this biblical book. These readings of text share a general category with the examples of ideological criticism referred to above. They wish to identify the undergirding of specific political reality by a defined programme of shaping and interpretation of chronological events which expresses the attitude of the community of origin, especially of the political elites of that society. In this context, Lena-Sofia Tiemeyer's paper argues that the themes of a renewed kingship and priestly class, found in Jeremiah, function to promote the continuation of a promise of power to a future ruling group.

As with Goldingay's volume, this volume of collected papers also retains an historical focus while engaging more recent reading methods in the service of that interest. While this scholarly volume retains a rooting in the historical discussions of earlier scholarship concerning history of composition, however, it acknowledges the uncertainty of more recent scholarship concerning the relevance of historical interpretations. The volume reveals that scholarship has gradually been moving from the search for historical certainties to an acknowledgement that written materials manage original events in ways that are shaped not only by writers and editors but also by political and cultural needs and uncertainties. The range of the collection comes into greater focus when set alongside an earlier volume of papers, edited by Adrian Curtis and Thomas Römer (1997). This book of essays is more centrally concerned with the questions of compositional history. Papers by John Applegate, Adrian Curtis, Jean-Daniel Macchi and Yohanan Goldman wrestle with the internal stages of development within the book of Jeremiah.

Applegate examines the link between doom messages and the hopeful sections of Jeremiah while Curtis explores the image of terror on every side in its Jeremianic usage, and Goldman looks to the evidence of MT/LXX versions. Where the volume moves beyond issues concerning the history of the composition of Jeremiah in its progress towards being part of a canonical Hebrew Bible is that it addresses the afterlife of the text in its reception by later communities. George Brooke reflects on Jeremiah at Qumran, and the later use of Jeremiah in 1 Corinthians and in the Gospel of Matthew is explored by Adrianjatovo Rakotoharintsifa and David Law. Pierluigi Piovanelli considers the re-use of Jeremiah material in the era of the Maccabees, while Roger Tomes reports on the reception of Jeremiah in Rabbinic literature and Jean-Daniel Kaestli on the influence of the book of Jeremiah in the *Paralipomena* of Jeremiah. In these papers, scholarship moves from the internal history of Jeremiah composition to the impact of the extant book on later audiences within Hellenistic and Roman times.

Having examined works of historical criticism at some length, it is possible to define historical scholarship in general as the intention to search for the meaning of a text through getting to know its original usage. The assumption is that to know the identity of the author or the timing of a passage allows the reader to access its *sitz im leben* (life-setting) and this in turn provides tools for interpretation, since any written material is intended by its author to respond to a particular issue or to communicate with a given audience. This authorial intention shapes the way in which words are used and what metaphors or idiomatic expressions are drawn down by the author from the vocabulary of their time. This approach is a thoroughly temporal one; it assumes that textual meaning is found in the traces of the past to be discovered in texts which have survived from previous cultures. In terms of Jeremiah studies, it has meant that the prophet's meaning is to be derived from the events of the late monarchy in Judah and from the final collapse of Jerusalem and an actual exile of leading figures from their territory.

Historical methodologies seek for the meaning of texts through defining their origins but the question is, can it be proved that the book of Jeremiah functions as this type of documentary material, as a deliberate work of history in its own right? Empirical study requires scholars to prove their views to be accurate by providing supportive evidence from outside the literary record, but there is little supporting evidence outside the Bible from which to flesh out chronological aspects of the life and times of Jeremiah (Mills 1999). It is clear that the text of Jeremiah places great weight on the themes of Exodus, Covenant and Exile but these terms can be defined from within the book for the part which they play within the political theology in which the material is engaged. How far the profile of a virtual Exile, for example, is synonymous with the events of the actual ethnic cleansing carried out by Assyrian and Babylonian rulers is a subject which has not been conclusively explained by historical scholarship of the twentieth century.

A further question can be asked at this point, which goes to the heart of the historical quest for understanding. It is easy to assume that ancient and modern audiences share a common definition of writing history. A work which addresses the temporal flow of events in modern culture is assumed to be one whose author has checked out factual details at some length and which does not assert the authenticity of the information it contains without this empirical approach to resource data. This approach to writing history does not completely rule out authorial bias on the part of the historian, but does provide a means of testing whether a given work is too subjective in its approach. Behind this is an assumption that ultimately history writers are seeking for 'the truth' about what happened in the past.

It is unclear how far ancient writers shared this post-Enlightenment European attitude to writing about the past. It is clear that biblical authors had a respect for past tradition and wished to make links between their present time and the traditional heritage. This can be seen in the works of two first-century CE Jewish writers whose works have survived. Both Philo of Alexandria and Josephus make use of the Pentateuchal traditions but the approach of each writer is quite different: whereas Josephus tells of the Antiquities of the Jews, Philo puts a philosophical interpretation on the patriarchal stories. Josephus prefers a narratival approach to tradition, re-telling traditional stories; Philo prefers to communicate the tradition in language drawn from the Greek schools of philosophical analysis.

It is perhaps better to speak of historiography than of history; the writing about past times which fully intends to draw out guidance for the current generation from ancestral tradition. It is in this context that scholarship has considered the possible links between the text of Jeremiah and the stylistics which govern the book of Deuteronomy and the books from Joshua to 2 Kings. Even so, there is a highly speculative side to making statements about who might have carried out such intertextual activity since ancient editors have not put their names to their work. Ultimately it is easier for scholars to pose historical questions about Jeremiah than it is for them to answer these queries convincingly.

As is noted in the volume edited by Diamond (1999), which will be discussed in Chapter 6, the fruits of a long period of historical research on Jeremiah emerged in the shape of a number of commentaries on the book written by scholars in the 1980s. These works mark a watershed in interpreting Jeremiah, each having their own way of explaining the historical roots of the creation of the book. A volume of Brueggemann's collected essays (2007) provides an evaluative summary of the field, commenting on the works of Ronald Clements, Robert Carroll, William McKane and William Holladay. Brueggemann notes that the last three of these commentaries were critical editions of scholarship which aimed at robust contributions to academic Jeremiah studies, while the book by Clements sets out to bring scholarship to bear on the task of preaching and teaching biblical material. All four, however, share a use of traditional modern methods of biblical exegesis and all focus on the person of Jeremiah, viewing the literary profile of the prophet as that of a creative genius. These commentaries brought together the suggestions of earlier scholars such as Duhm and Mowinckel and the nuancing of their arguments by individual pieces of research such as those addressed earlier in this chapter.

Holladay and McKane share a similar style in that they provide detailed scrutiny of the text. Holladay's aim is to construct the historical career of

Jeremiah from within the contents of the prophetic book, a project which he believes to be viable; McKane focuses on the growth of textual materials and employs strict linguistic analysis to carry out his task of identifying additions to an original edition of the writings of Jeremiah. These parallel methodologies exemplify the two major concerns of historical critics— to establish the life and times of the prophet and to work out an accurate account of the historical composition of the final book.

Each in his own way, Clements and Carroll also address basically historical models of exegesis. Clements is mainly concerned with the use of Jeremiah in pastoral activity so wants to provide suitable resources for this task. The rationale for his study is the avoidance of technical detail and the focus on how the original audience would have encountered the prophetic writings, a subject which provides a bridge to how a modern audience can receive the text in the context of itself functioning as preacher and teacher of tradition. Carroll's work is historical in intention but breaks with scholarship in that it looks not to the political context of an earlier prophet but to the setting of the final exilic audience as the tool for understanding the book's contents. This commentary style is ambiguous, Brueggemann suggests, since it denies an interest in historical modes of exegesis while in fact looking for meaning through historical contextualization.

For Brueggemann, none of these modern works of scholarship adequately addresses the relationship of an ancient book to a modern audience adequately. In fact he is concerned that there is no obvious alignment of academic scholarly concerns with the needs of a readership which is interested in the theological contents of Jeremiah. He critiques the so-called objectivity of an historical approach as subjective, in that it implies theology is not a suitable topic for biblical scholarship. Scholarship has become detached from everyday life, he suggests; what is needed is a new approach which he sees as emerging from less stress on the Deuteronomic editing of Jeremiah and a reading of the book from the angle of creation theology, a method of reading set out in the writings of Leo Perdue. In this context Brueggemann explores Jer. 4.24-29 with its image of God as agent of creation. Creation theology highlights the links between creation and soteriology since all beings are objects of divine activity from start to finish. This establishes an essential I-Thou relationship between God and world, as noted in the work of Martin Buber and Emmanuel Levinas, and which gives a rationale for preaching and teaching biblical texts for a wider audience than academic scholarship.

In order to move the work of interpretation on in fruitful ways, Brueggemann suggests that there needs to be a retreat from the detachment from living audiences, which has come to characterize historical research, and a turn towards rhetorical strategies, which a text follows in order to communicate its religious message. In terms of the book of Jeremiah this means giving attention to the multiple voices of the text, voices that are shrill, disjunctive and conflicting. It is in this form of exegesis that the voice of transcendence may be heard, Brueggemann argues. In voicing these opinions, Brueggemann's evaluation of the state of Jeremiah studies in the mid-1980s foreshadows the movement to a fully rhetorical mode of reading which developed in the 1990s and beyond. In its desire to have academic research serve practical theological needs, the chapter exemplifies Brueggemann's own contribution to the study of Jeremiah, a topic which will be returned to in Chapter 8 below.

Having summarized Brueggemann's overview, it is possible to look in more detail at some of the points he raises with regard to these commentaries. In what way are the volumes by Holladay and McKane traditional, for example? The answer to this question is that each in their own way stresses that textual meaning emerges from looking into the historical origins of Jeremiah. In his preface to the first volume, Holladay states that he is addressing himself to technical issues in translating the Hebrew text and will keep close to the original language version of the book (MT) in providing an English edition. At the same time, he notes that he has made comparative studies of ancient material where this could illuminate a reader's understanding; in this regard Holladay examined Ugaritic materials and also fragments of Jeremiah found at Qumran.

This makes his commentary a detailed and highly academic work; by using such careful methodology, Holladay aims to construct the timing of the historical prophet's career and hence the immediate settings for his words. He makes this construction in line with proposing that the date 627 BCE marks the birth of the prophet, not the start of his career. This makes Jeremiah five years old when King Josiah carried out his reforms and since the law was to be read publicly every seven years it is possible to give a timeframe for the oracles in chaps. 1–25—as historical speeches made by Jeremiah at these times. While, according to Holladay, Jeremiah is a difficult book to analyse, the scholar can use the biographical slant of the prophetic book as a documentary resource, while also addressing the book's profile in other ancient language versions.

This mode of interpretation is very much one of traditional historical criticism and close attention to detail is manifest also in McKane's work. His commentary is more technical even than Holladay's and takes a fully linguistic approach to tracing additions to the original core of Jeremiah. By analysing comparative vocabulary within the book of Jeremiah and in language versions such as the LXX and the Syriac versions of the material, McKane aims to demonstrate how words and concepts were used and re-used, with the Deuteronomic aspects of chaps. 1–25 providing a foundation for finding extensions to meaning which underpin the gradual growth of insertions and additions to the original core. McKane finds that the views of his fellow commentators sometimes fail to address the complexity of this textual development, by attributing a great deal to the work of Baruch, for instance. Rather than being able to identify separate sources, the commentator can only talk of a slow but continuous process by which an original core was expanded to make the current book.

Carroll's commentary is also a detailed analysis of the text of Jeremiah but Carroll states that he wishes to remove himself from the historical discussions of origins which previous scholars have carried out. Carroll argues that this way of operating cannot arrive at clear answers about the prophetic book's message. His study works from a fully redactional stance and considers the situation of the group who produced the edited form of the book in the exilic/postexilic period. Carroll believes that the historical profile of Jeremiah disappears behind the viewpoints of the editors of the material and that it is not possible to find out the names of any specific editors of the book. He takes up the arguments of Ernest Nicholson that the figure of the prophet functions as a paradigmatic character, a preacher to exiles. The editors deliberately created a literary persona which is pluralist. Jeremiah speaks both for and against Babylon, acting as prophet not only to Judah but to the nations. Jeremiah is a conglomerate of conflicting views held by members of the community which was the intended audience.

In this approach, Carroll moved to examining the book of Jeremiah as a whole, a work which can be read synchronically rather than by being split into sections by genre and by dating of composition. This approach shows traces of the move to rhetorical criticism, which was emerging at this time in Jeremiah studies, but Carroll's critics point out that his perspective does not ultimately avoid an historical approach to text—it simply re-situates historical issues to the endpoint of the making of the book. At the same time as Carroll is rejecting earlier historical criticism, he stresses the significance of an objective methodology which respects the gap between the ancient past and a modern readership, condemning interpretations which prioritize modern concerns such as the role of women as well as those which focus on confessional, faith-based meanings.

These three scholarly works serve to illustrate the achievements and the problems of historical approaches to the book of Jeremiah. They demonstrate that it is correct to view the book as the result of a long period of redaction but also show how difficult it is to arrive at the goal of historical research, namely clear and compelling arguments for the authorship, date and setting of the book's contents. They make the point that in the end it is the literary work itself which modern readers have to deal with, its contents and literary structures. Their work also raises the question of how far any reader of an ancient book can have access to the mind-set of a very different society in its own right, excluding the possibility of being influenced by the interests of one's own cultural context. Recognition of this truth has led to the gradual move to a self-aware reading of Jeremiah in which modern issues are owned as the location from which ancient texts are examined.

Given the validity of raising historical questions, and the difficulty of providing compelling answers to those questions, it is perhaps not surprising that Jeremiah scholarship began to turn more fully to the use of literary theory to examine the textual poetics which are present within the final text of Jeremiah. In particular, scholars focused on the rhetorical power of the material. As with the historical methods, a close reading of the text remained at the centre of interpretation but interest was less on the situations which lie behind the book of Jeremiah in their own right and more on the textual expression of responses made by ancient writers to those social, political and religious contexts.

## *Further Reading/References*

Applegate, John
   1997   'Peace, peace, when there is no peace', in Curtis and Römer (1997): 51-90.
   1997   'Jeremiah and the Seventy Years in the Hebrew Bible', in Curtis and Römer (1997): 91-110.
Auld, Graeme
   2009   'Jeremiah–Manasseh–Samuel, Significant Triangle?', in Barstad and Kratz (2009): 1-9.
Barstad, Hans
   2009   'What Prophets Do: Reflections on Past Realities in the Book of Jeremiah', in Barstad and Kratz (2009): 10-32.
Barstad, Hans and Reinhard Kratz (eds.)
   2009   *Prophecy in the Book of Jeremiah* (Berlin: de Gruyter).
Boadt, Lawrence
   2007   'Do Jeremiah and Ezekiel Share a Common View of the Exile?', in Goldingay (2007): 14-31.
Brooke, George
   1997   'The Book of Jeremiah and its Reception in the Qumran Scrolls', in Curtis and Römer (1997): 183-206.
Brueggemann, W. (ed. P.D. Miller)
   2007   *Like Fire in the Bones: Listening for the Prophetic Word in Jeremiah* (Minneapolis: Fortress Press).
Buber, Martin
   2013   *I and Thou* (London: Bloomsbury).
Carroll, R.
   1986   *Jeremiah* (London: SCM Press).
Chavel, S.
   1997   'Let my People Go! Emancipation, Revelation and Scribal Activity in Jer. 34:8-14', *JSOT* 76: 71-95.
Clements, R.
   1988   *Jeremiah* (Atlanta: John Knox Press).
Collins, Terence
   1997   'Deuteronomist Influence on the Prophetical Books', in Curtis and Römer (1997): 15-26.
Curtis, Adrian
   1997   'Terror on every side!', in Curtis and Römer (1997): 111-18.

Curtis, A., and T. Römer (eds.)
  1997    *The Book of Jeremiah and its Reception* (Leuven: Peeters).
Diamond, P. (ed.)
  1999    *Troubling Jeremiah* (London: T. & T. Clark International).
Domeris, William
  2007    'Jeremiah and the Poor', in Goldingay (2007): 45-58.
Duhm, B.
  1901    *Das Buch Jeremia* (Tübingen: Mohr).
Gladon, Jerry
  2001    'Jeremiah 17:19-27: A Rewriting of the Sinaitic Code?', *CBQ* 62: 33-40.
Goldingay, J. (ed.)
  2007    *Uprooting and Planting: Essays on Jeremiah for Leslie Allen* (London: T. & T. Clark International).
Goldman, Yohannan
  1997    'Juda et son roi au milieu des nations: la dernière rédaction du livre de Jérémie', in Curtis and Römer (1997): 151-82.
Grabbe, Lester
  2009    'Jeremiah among the Social Anthropologists', in Barstad and Kratz (2009): 80-88.
Hill, John
  2007    'The Book of Jeremiah and its Second Temple Background', in Goldingay (2007): 153-71.
Holladay, W. L.
  1986    *Jeremiah*, Vol. 1 (Philadelphia: Fortress Press).
  1989    *Jeremiah*, Vol. 2 (Minneapolis: Fortress Press).
  2001    'Had Ezekiel Known Jeremiah Personally', *CBQ* 63: 31-34.
Jong, M. de
  2011a   'True and False Prophecy: Jeremiah's Revision of Deuteronomy', *JSOT* 35: 339-58.
  2011b   'Why Jeremiah is Not Among the Prophets: An Analysis of the Terms נביא and נבאים in the Book of Jeremiah', *JSOT* 35: 483-510.
Kaestli, Jean-Daniel
  1997    'L'Influence du live de Jeremie dans les Paralipomenes de Jeremie', in Curtis and Romer (1997): 217-32.
Lee, Nancy
  2007    'Prophet and Sage in the Fray: The Book of Jeremiah', in Goldingay (2007): 190-209.
Leuchter, M.
  2005    'The Temple Sermon and the Term לקום in the Jeremianic Corpus', *JSOT* 30: 93-109.
  2008    *The Polemics of Exile in Jeremiah 26–45* (Cambridge: Cambridge University Press).
Levinas, Emmanuel
  1985    *Ethics and Infinity* (Pittsburgh, PA: Duquesne University Press).
Lundberg, Marilyn
  2007    'The Mis-Pi Rituals and Incantation in Jeremiah 10:1-16', in Goldingay (2007): 210-27.
Macchi, Jean-Louis
  1997    'Les doublets dans le livre de Jérémie', in Curtis and Römer (1997): 119-50.

McKane, W.
 1986  *Jeremiah*, vol. 1 (Edinburgh: T. & T. Clark).
 1996  *Jeremiah*, vol. 2 (Edinburgh: T. & T. Clark).
Mills, M.
 1999  *Historical Israel: Biblical Israel* (London: Cassell).
Moore, Michael
 2007  'The Lamentation in Jeremiah and 1QH', in Goldingay (2007): 228-52.
Mowinckel, S.
 1914  *Zur Komposition des Buches Jeremia* (Oslo: Jacob Dybwad).
Nissinen, Martti
 2009  'The Historical Dilemma of Biblical Prophetic Studies', in Barstad and Kratz
       (2009): 103-120.
Overholt, T.
 1992  *Cultural Anthropology and the Old Testament* (Augsburg: Fortress Press).
Perdue, Leo G.
 2001  *Wisdom and Creation: The Theology of Wisdom Literature* (New York: Wipf
       & Stock).
 2007  'Baruch among the Sages...', in Goldingay (2007): 260-90.
Rakotoharintsifa, Andrianjatovo
 1997  'Jérémie en action au Corinthe', in Curtis and Römer (1997): 207-16.
Reimer, David
 2009  'Redeeming Politics in Jeremiah', in Barstad and Kratz (2009): 121-36.
Römer, Thomas
 1997  'La conversion du prophète Jérémie à la théologie deuteronomiste', in Curtis
       and Römer (1997): 27-50.
Schaper, Joachim
 2009  'On Reading and Reciting in Jeremiah 36', in Barstad and Kratz (2009):
       127-47.
Sharp, C.
 2000  'The Call of Jeremiah and Diaspora Politics', *JBL* 119: 421-38.
Sommer, B.
 1999  'New Light on the Composition of Jeremiah', *CBQ* 61: 646-66.
Tiemeyer, Lena-Sofia
 2009  'The Priests and Temple Cult in the Book of Jeremiah', in Barstad and Kratz
       (2009): 233-64.
Watts, J.
 1992  'Text and Redaction in Jeremiah's Oracles against the Nations', *CBQ* 54:
       432-47.
Weeks, Stuart
 2009  'Jeremiah as a Prophetic Book', in Barstad and Kratz (2009): 265-74.
Wells, Roy
 2007  'Dislocation in Time and Ideology in the Reconception of Jeremiah's Words...',
       in Goldingay (2007): 322-50.
Williams, M.
 1993  'An Investigation of the Legitimacy of Source Distinctions for the Prose
       Material in Jeremiah', *JBL* 112: 193-210.

For works of Philo and Josephus see the *Loeb Classics* series.

Chapter 5

THE MOVE TO RHETORICAL CRITICISM

By the late 1980s, the major strands of historical criticism of the book of Jeremiah had been identified and essential questions posed. The process of history of interpretation tended to stress the fundamentally fragmentary nature of the book and break the contents into independent units based on the history of composition. A temporal approach looked always to the past, to the creation and re-writing of material in the light of ancient societies and their cultural concerns. The failure to reach consensus on the origins of the book, and the fragmentation in meaning resulting from identifying the individuality of sub-sections within the text, led to a shift in focus to the final editors of Jeremiah and their redactional strategies. This, in turn, led scholars to engage with the rhetorical structure of the final book in the search for meaning, even though this also involved acceptance of the fragmentary shape of the biblical work as part of that redactional framework. A move to focus more on textual construction led to an interest in Jeremiah's use of metaphor and in the shaping of characters and of plot.

This chapter traces the rise of rhetorical criticism as an important contribution to the interpretation of the book of Jeremiah. Study of the rhetorical shape of a text focuses on what is 'in the text', on language, vocabulary and poetic devices such as metaphor and dramatic irony. In this approach, the text is regarded as a symbolic world which reflects the actual historical world behind the text but has its own individual identity. In the historical world of late monarchy and the rise of Mesopotamian empires, Jerusalem and its temple was a focus for Judahite culture, religion and politics. These real life institutions of socio-political life had their own profile but equally they are sites of plot action within the book of Jeremiah. Their function within the book provides Jerusalem, the temple, Babylon and Egypt (to name the major places referred to) with a textual profile within the symbolic universe of Jeremiah. In Jeremiah 7, for example, the historical role of the temple as a site of public worship associated with the indwelling presence of the deity is utilized to give the setting for a message which confounds complacent religious activity; trusting that, because a deity has been attached to a geographical site in the past, the cultic centre is protected forever is an illusion.

The new area of scholarly interest in literary style opened up as a result partly of the work of the Society of Biblical Literature Consultation on the Composition of Jeremiah unit. This fresh approach focused increasingly on the topic of rhetorical style, on how text makes its impact on readership. The 1999 volume, *Troubling Jeremiah*, edited by Pete Diamond, Kathleen O'Connor and Louis Stulman provides an access point to the considerations of that programme unit in its work of opening up the field of rhetorical criticism since it emerged as an offshoot of scholarly collaboration within the workings of the Society for Biblical Literature. Diamond and like-minded researchers were ready to ask whether there were any new approaches to understanding Jeremiah which scholarship had not as yet developed—which led to a focus on literary stylistics and how the text makes an impact on readers.

A useful introduction to the shift in interpretive paradigm in Jeremiah studies is found in Diamond's editorial essay in *Troubling Jeremiah* since this aims to set out the field of Jeremiah studies to which the papers within the volume contribute. Diamond notes how scholars constantly disagree about which are the more appropriate methods of studying the book, covering historical method, literary readings and reader-centred approaches, and argues that any over-arching theological meaning cannot ignore the individuality of interpretation produced across such a varied range of reading methods. To frame the debate, Diamond suggests that students take as a starting point the late 1980s, as this period marks both an end and a beginning, shaped as it was by the appearance of notable commentaries on Jeremiah: works by Carroll, Holladay, McKane, Overholt, Brueggemann and Clements. These commentaries, which were discussed in the previous chapter, mark the climax of the work begun by earlier scholars such as Duhm and Mowinckel.

These volumes, Diamond suggests, are important because they gather together the fruits of the historical-critical approaches to Jeremiah which had emerged during the twentieth century. They demonstrate the range of interpretation produced by an historical method, since all apply an historical lens to reading the text but each writer has a very different understanding of what the use of historical tools tells the reader about the nature of the book. Diamond notes, for instance, the shift from focusing on the life and times of a pre-exilic era political figure as central to understanding the book to Carroll's angle of examining post-exilic socio-political conditions as the production context. In the first mode of exegesis, the book of Jeremiah is viewed as reflecting a literary tradition which looks back to a founding figure and it is in the voice of that figure that meaning is found. In Carroll's work, Jeremiah is assumed to be a book which emerged in a post-exilic world and which has been shaped by the needs of that culture, especially with regard to re-grouping religious belief in the wake of a major political disaster.

The common feature of all these commentators, however, is their stress on the compositional history of the biblical work; by contrast the new approach to studying Jeremiah is to take the book in its entirety as a piece of literature and to explore the features of its literary construction in terms of modern critical theories. In simple terms, this entails moving from what lies behind the text to what is in the text, as well as considering who may stand in front of the text—the nature of audiences with whom the book of Jeremiah communicates. It is useful to note here Diamond's summary of a shift in scholarly attention to the treatment of the symbolic imagined world of the text as constituting a viable hermeneutical base (19-27).

Here Diamond emphasizes the need to take a book seriously in its own right and to look for the meaning of that text through consideration of its vocabulary, grammar and poetic devices such as characterization, plot and time and place settings. A synchronic approach to biblical literature is deepened when it draws on the methodology of modern literary criticism and Diamond notes in this regard the value of engaging with modern critical theory, such as found in the work of Ferdinand de Saussure's examination of the foundational structures of literary language and the post-structuralist critique of his linguistic theories. The adoption of exegetical techniques drawn from literary theory which in turn stresses the importance of literature as a means of human communication, where language is viewed as having inbuilt codes of usage which pre-exist everyday oral speech, provides the biblical interpreter with specific exegetical tools, applicable to any serious work of literature.

Focusing on the interior world of the text is a methodology which is not without its own interest in the culture with which the text engages in its production of meaning. Since texts are written to communicate with an audience and to persuade readers to embrace their message, they cannot be treated as simple verbal productions, innocent of a pre-determined intention with regard to social impact. It is important, therefore, to consider the nature of the symbolic world which is found inside a book. Diamond refers at this point to the view of Carroll that the entire tenor of Jeremiah is deconstructive: that the author/editors tend to use symbol systems familiar to an ancient audience in order to undermine the sense of familiarity and security these systems produce. As noted above with regard to the use of temple symbolism in chap. 7, the book of Jeremiah mediates its message of doom through picturing key institutional realities—state cult and royal household—which are normally taken for granted, as under threat of erasure. The major symbols reshaped by the prophet go to the heart of cultural identity since they include the dominant state religion and the *mythos* of divine sovereignty.

Consideration of the imaginative world created within a piece of literature leads on to the issue of whom the text is communicating with and what impact is intended on that readership. The focus shifts from composition and literary style to readers and their potential responses to texts, since texts are produced to influence readers to accept particular worldviews. No text is 'innocent' suggests Diamond, indicating that every piece of literature carries a coded evaluation of daily life which it seeks to persuade readers to accept. In this setting, literature is to be seen as a tool for gaining power over audiences: hence books have ideological shaping. This is a viewpoint which was raised above in Chapter 4, where attention was drawn to Goldingay's account of Jeremiah's imperialistic language as a tool of ideological activity. Diamond's editorial essay notes that a relevant modern field of study for understanding ideological criticism is that of social theory of literature; in this context a reader needs to focus on the socio-political goal of any given book.

In applying this critical tool to Jeremiah, it has to be noted that since this book is polyphonic, made up of a number of genres each with its own individual 'voice' contributing to the overall message of the book, only after due attention has been given to the tendency of individual elements of Jeremiah to contradict and oppose each other can the final synchronic verdict on the overall socio-religious message of the book be made. Any such theological interpretation will still need to incorporate the diversity and fragmentation evidenced within the book. In her essay, O'Connor exemplifies this mode of working by arguing that the book produces a theology of the divine character as non-unified, de-stabilized and multiple, constructed from the imagery of husband, general, and lamenting voice. She suggests that what holds these images together is a concept based on the thematic unity between them, which can be called 'divine tears' and which conveys an ideology of the inevitable collapse of the central systems of government.

Diamond has edited the collection of essays in *Troubling Jeremiah* via three interpretive methods—text-centred, reader-centred, theology-centred—which each flesh out an aspect of a rhetorical investigation of Jeremiah. In the section on textual stylistics, it is the symbolic world of the book which is examined while the reader-centred section shows an awareness of modern views on gender issues as a reading lens for ancient texts. The concern with actual modern readers of Jeremiah opens out into the reading location as 'in front of the text', with its concern for the particular responses of different audiences to the same text. Only after dealing with the inherently fragmented nature of the book does this volume of essays return to the project of defining the overall theological message of the material contained under the umbrella name of Jeremiah.

In the text-centred section, there is recognition of the divisions of subsections of Jeremiah material produced by source and form criticism but there is also a move towards looking at the signs of redactional activity in the final text, leading to consideration of the rhetorical strategies at work therein. Stulman, for example, uses the prose sermons as a hermeneutical guide to the whole of Jeremiah 1–25, suggesting that these passages focalize the message of the chapters as a depiction of a world deconstructed, as with Jeremiah 7 and 11, for instance, as explained in Chapter 2 above. Martin Kessler examines the holistic nature of the book by arguing that Jeremiah 25, 50 and 51 are used as three pillars in its construction. In each of these chapters Babylon's supremacy is referred to—positively in Jer. 25.8-11 and negatively in Jeremiah 50–51. Within the text of Jeremiah, he suggests, the city-state of Babylon functions as a pivotal symbol which governs both the earlier message of the ending of the past life of Judah and the message of its restoration following Babylon's own demise.

Attention has already been drawn in the historical-criticism chapters above to the importance of examining the intertextuality of Jeremiah with other biblical works. A further form of intertextuality relates to the rhetorical links between literary works, such as the use of wordplay and common metaphors. In this context, Nancy Lee explores possible intertextuality between the Cain and Abel story in Genesis 4 and accusations against Judah in Jeremiah; In Jer. 14.10 for instance the people 'wander'—a word play on the root C-N and a reference to the curse on Cain to be a wanderer with everyone's hand against him.

Intertextual links between separate books is a topic addressed again in the reader-centred section of these collected essays, where Carroll uses an approach derived from the literary theory of Mikhail Bakhtin concerning textual polyphony and applies it to the writers of the 'Book of J' with its intertextual links to Deuteronomy and Joshua–Kings. Carroll's analysis examines the way in which the presence of Deuteronomic echoes in a wider book produces narrative voices which dialogue with each other within a single work. While these essays deal with overlaps across books, Alice Bellis examines intertextual links within Jeremiah itself. She explores Jeremiah 50 with its three separate but interlocking poems on the fall of Babylon, arguing that they share a common theme of justice (via Babylon) and mercy (via Judah's pardon) which is the literary device holding the whole chapter together. Bellis introduces this treatment by dividing the material of chap. 50 into three individual poems: vv. 2-17, 18b-32, 33-46, which each denounce Babylon.

Further interpretive methods can be extracted from rhetorical analysis, all of which highlight the significance of linguistic devices such as imagery or the creation of narrative passages within Jeremiah. Else Holt's contribution utilizes narrative criticism, by which tool she investigates Jeremiah 37–44 as a form of short novella, looking at how characterization, plot and settings shape these chapters and thus construct meaning. In this section of text, the scene is set with the reign of Zedekiah within which Jeremiah speaks and acts at the royal court. The prophet's enemies and supporters are brought into the plot and the section closes with the exiles fleeing to Egypt as Jeremiah comments on their actions.

John Hill focuses on the use of symbolic language to construct meaning. He identifies the symbolic use of time in Jeremiah 25, arguing that the scope of time—past, present and future—is used symbolically to identify the present time of the chapter as a period of waiting between past temporal events and an indefinite future hope for restoration. The motif of divine sending of prophets is highlighted since the deity has sent a stream of prophets who have not been listened to by the people. God will send Nebuchadnezzar in the future and will arrange a time of liberation after 70 years. The two time-settings, past and future, focus the reader on the present unstable and doomed time of Judahite kingship.

Issues of language usage appear also in Diamond and O'Connor's work on gendered imagery in Jeremiah, an iconography which nuances the power of symbolic language in conveying meaning to readers. They ask what happens when powerful symbols inserted into ancient texts no longer communicate the original sense of the writer because the imagery itself is under suspicion in the minds of a later audience, as with female images in Scripture today. Gendered imagery has become a matter for close scrutiny in biblical texts, as the interest in rhetorical criticism and the impact of literature on real audiences has grown in strength. In the second section of the volume, Angela Bauer also explores the function of female imagery in Jeremiah. She argues that gendered voices are deliberately used to express the book's meaning which means that the divine voice is contextualized by sounds of war and the voices of women in lament at the results of battle.

The emphasis on symbolic language as a tool of communication raises issues of currency of language and leads into consideration of reader response to texts. Audiences provide a plurality of interpretive concepts for Jeremiah studies. Mary Calloway, for instance, uses the response to the book which emerged from Rabbinic Judaism to emphasize the need not to subdue the tensions between subsections of text noted by historical criticism. Rather, the variety of meaning so provided is to be embraced as it stands, taking Jeremiah seriously as a complex and layered book. This complexity is strengthened by serious investigation of the audiences of the biblical work, who come from varied backgrounds and have individual interests in possible meanings.

William Domeris contributes to this approach from the angle of sociolinguistics, a reading lens which demonstrates how a person's social location shapes the range of vocabulary and concepts available for expressing ideas, since language is embedded in the culture to which it gives voice. Domeris links a socio-linguistic approach to the topic of ideological criticism, noting not only that mainstream culture produces dominant ideological perspectives but that anti-language within a text can counter the establishment view. He argues that Jeremiah may be viewed as the work of a group with an anti-society intention, using language to overthrow one political ideology with another; this dynamic could be used to explain the literary profile of Hananiah and Jeremiah in Jeremiah 28, material addressed above.

Raymond Person Jr focuses on the issue of reception of texts by audiences as he states that the reception of a book is a cultural affair. Person uses this angle to critique modern scholarship's approach, comparing this body of comment with the views of ancient audiences of Jeremiah. History of composition studies which examine the development of LXX and MT can go astray, precisely because they forefront the written nature of tradition, he says. Ancient cultures carried knowledge by oral methods in which the variants between versions of the same material were much less important than the preservation of the main teaching.

Cultural issues also interest Roy Wells, who addresses the meaning of Jeremiah as a MT book. Whereas historical scholars centred their work on the evidence for compositional history provided by the MT version, Wells sees in the MT edition of Jeremiah the vested interests of the survivors of the Babylonian invasions and the political self-justification of the generation which restored Judah under Persian rule. Meanwhile, John Barton's essay on how Jeremiah was shaped by, and itself shaped, later readers in texts from the Apocrypha and Pseudepigrapha reinforces the need to examine not only what led to the emergence of early material but also how the tradition once in existence contributes to cultural searches for meaning across many centuries. In this context, Barton explores the afterlife of Jeremiah in authors from Josephus to 4 Baruch, to 4 Ezra, to Eusebius.

The variability of meaning and the mutual impact of text and reader make the entreprise of defining the theology of Jeremiah an ambivalent task. The theology section of the volume edited by Diamond engages with the controversial nature of constructing 'the' theology of Jeremiah. Leo Perdue sets out the cultural context of modern society with its collapse of metanarratives and scepticism of history as source of meaning. Despite this contemporary distrust of metanarrative, Perdue seeks out a paradigm for theological investigation drawn from biblical scholarship—from creation theology to narrative theology to the use of imaginative theology—applying each to the contents of Jeremiah. Dennis Olsen and Overholt critique Perdue's approach, which seems to balance between affirming pluralism and driving towards coherence.

This debate illustrates the ambivalence felt in modern scholarship towards the project of extracting a single theology from a biblical work which is, as Calloway noted, sprawling and fragmented. Other essays in the theological section of *Troubling Jeremiah* manage this problematic context either from a preference for a sense of cohesion or for difference. Whereas Brueggemann finds a link between history and theology in Jeremiah in the figure of a scribal Baruch, who lived alongside events which were then transformed into an ideological tool, shaped by the Deuteronomic editors and carrying the imprint of their religio-political views, O'Connor embraces the individuality of different parts of the book, whose only unifying theme is that of a 'weeping deity'.

Returning, then, to the topic of the emergent methods in Jeremiah studies after the 1980s, the analysis of Diamond's edited volume offered above establishes the range of parallel reading methods which have emerged within the last 30 years and which involve a focus either on textual poetics or on reader reception of existing texts. The volume of essays indicates that there is both divergence and similarity between historical and rhetorical schools of biblical studies. Diamond's group of writers acknowledge the weight of past scholarship in providing perspectives on the history of composition but strive to move beyond that focus to newer reading methodologies and the meaning that emerges from using these methods to read Jeremiah. It is, however, the same final text which is being read, whether diachronically or synchronically, and so there is, for instance, a commonality of concern with the themes of pain and suffering by which most of the book of Jeremiah is shaped.

Comparing the essays found in the Goldingay volume discussed in Chapter 4 above with those in the Diamond volume it can be seen how far both historical and rhetorical critics of Jeremiah share an interest in the same topics and how the specific reading method used produces different contributions to understanding the text. Domeris, for example, has material in both volumes but his contribution to the Goldingay volume attaches a focus on socio-linguistics to the possible agricultural context of the original audience of Jeremiah, whereas his essay in Diamond's volume stresses the relevance of methods drawn from critical theory in a wider sense. In the historical approach, the reading lens of socio-linguistics is acknowledged but only to pass beyond theory to a specific case study which illustrates how the actual agricultural life style of an ancient city state provides material for metaphorical comments on politics at that time. In his other essay, Domeris reflects on the nature of critical theory in its own right. This entails considering the shape of the rhetorical methodology, its range and functions before identifying how this linguistic reading lens could be applied to biblical exegesis as a deliberate choice for a preferred method. Domeris' style here models an exegetical practice which has become widespread in the twenty-first century.

As Diamond notes, rhetorical study does not drive out historical meaning but rather adds parallel strands of interpretation; indeed Diamond himself, together with Stulman and O'Connor, began research into meaning in Jeremiah from within historical critical schools of academic study. Diamond had already begun to move towards a synchronic approach to reading Jeremiah in his treatment of the Confessions of Jeremiah in context (1987) since this study moves from exegesis of individual passages to consider their inter-relationship. Diamond fits this approach within the historical-critical focus on the history of composition, especially with regard to the Deuter-onomic level of editing, stressing its individuality, but then moves on to consider the function of the individual passages within their immediate lit-erary context—an exegetical perspective which balances between historical and rhetorical approaches.

This balancing of older methodology with fresh attention to the book as literature can be seen in John Job's book on Jeremiah's Kings. Job writes that he wants to examine the indictment of rulers from the context of regional events of the ancient Near East rather than from the affectiv-ity angle put forward by Timothy Polk. Jeremiah is a prophet of exile, a character shaped by the references in the symbolic textual world to ancient battles and political upheavals. There is good archaeological evidence that invasion and imperialism were indeed the avowed intention of Assyrian forces and so close reading of the judgments made on kings from Josiah to Zedekiah can be set against the external record of invasion and this study can then be used to enhance the redaction critic's contribution to the com-positional history of Jeremiah. Understanding of the historical dimension to interpretation of Jeremiah is enhanced when set alongside works which deal with the symbolic textual world in its own right—works such as that by Timothy Polk, whose book on the prophetic persona (1984) provides a second early witness to the shift of scholarly interest from exploring possi-ble history behind the text to analysing the methods of textual construction.

Polk's study moves between historical and rhetorical methods as he notes the high profile given to the prophetic figure in Jeremiah and contextualizes this in relation to the dual image of historic figure and literary persona. He comments on the reconstructions of the historical figure made by scholars such as John Skinner but critiques this type of study as a form of diachronic investigation which is balanced by synchronic readings of the final book as a whole; he supports his arguments by appeal to the structuralist method-ology of the French theorist de Saussure. Structuralism provides a critical method which seeks to identify the 'laws' by which written communication is properly constructed.

By this move, Polk relocates the endeavour to create a biography of the historical Jeremiah to an exploration of the ways in which the language of the text expresses a concept of selfhood. Polk applies this model of the self to exegesis of the biblical work and draws out the text's usage of the heart as metaphor for personal experience. Within the Confessions passages Jer-emiah acts as exemplar, becoming himself a metaphor for communal expe-rience. Polk's work showed that while the historical search for the prophet had not produced a clear prophetic identity it was still possible to explore the significance of the prophet from within the linguistic contents of the book, revealing the function of his persona to act as a symbol of trusting piety, held up to the readership of the tradition.

Diamond and Polk share a common stylistic, in that they move from historical to rhetorical interests, while maintaining the framework of seg-mented units of the book of Jeremiah resulting from history of composition research. A different rhetorical approach is found in the book by Kelvin Froe-bel (1999) which explores non-verbal rhetorical communication. Froebel sets out a model of non-verbal communication first before interpreting prophetic sign-acts in Jeremiah and Ezekiel. In this approach, the scholar locates an aspect of modern theory, explaining the shape of this theoretical approach before applying it as a reading lens to biblical books. The theoretical model is employed alongside detailed exegesis of the construction of passages from the Hebrew text and the ancient text is viewed from within the methodology which has been used by the commentator. Evaluation of the text and its mean-ing is in this way shaped by the concerns of the modern world. It has already been noted in this chapter how this type of methodology compares and con-trasts with an historical focus, as evidenced by the work of Domeris.

Froebel argues that the basic characterization of Jeremiah depicts the prophet as having appropriate communication and rhetorical skills, allow-ing for modern analytical tools to be applied to the book's contents. He clar-ifies the nature of the tools of the model to be applied to interpret the text by stating that the use of non-verbal channels of communication does not derive from the inherently efficacious nature of the actions but from the ability of the non-verbal form of communication to dramatize meaning and so to highlight the specific message to be conveyed. Non-verbal skills sit alongside verbal skills of communication and function as rhetorical vehi-cles to address the theological matters with which an audience is concerned. They can be adjusted to deliver messages both of judgment and of hope and thus link to the history of invasion, loss and restoration which defines the political background of the book of Jeremiah.

Froebel takes as case study Jeremiah's contest with Hananiah which highlights the role which sign-acts play in articulating conflicted messages. The two men are in contest not over the validity of prophetic activity in its own right but with regard to a particular oracle. Both prophets agree that God is capable of breaking the yoke of foreign control; in Jer. 30.8 Jere-miah is viewed as the giver of a true message in which God will break the yoke, as set against his view in chap. 28 that the yoke is here to stay. But they differ in terms of what they think God will do in the immediate polit-ical context under debate. Since Jeremiah 28 reveals how deeply aligned the Judahite belief system was with the inviolability of kingship and temple cult, any shift in belief systems would be an act of cognitive dissonance and so strongly resisted by the audience. It is within this framework that non-verbal behaviour is to be interpreted, as the viable means of illustrating the size of the challenge to establishment norms proposed by Jeremiah him-self. The wearing and the breaking of a yoke on the part of the two equally 'valid' prophets provides a sign-act sequence which dramatizes the conflicting choices faced by those participating in this biblical scene.

Froebel's study is an example of a method which becomes increasingly present in contemporary work on the text of Jeremiah. Reading methods are drawn from modern critical theory with regard to linguistics, to social theories of literature and to gender-related topics. The scholar identifies the aspect of critical theory in its own right and then creates from that basis a reading lens through which to approach the biblical material. This mode of working does not entirely negate an historical dimension to the text but chooses to investigate what fresh meaning can be found via the interrogation of the text from the vantage point of critical analysis which can be applied to literature as such.

Other scholars interested in rhetorical structures had already approached this topic through an historical lens. Jack Lundbom (1975) for example, examined the literary structure of the Jeremiah text, its use of *inclusion* and *chiasmus*, as a medium for refining arguments both in source criticism of Jeremiah and form-critical perspectives on the material. He argued that gaining clarity with regard to the limits and borders of units of tradition is a vital tool for developing the compositional history of the book. Meanwhile, Mark Smith, writing on the lament passages in Jeremiah, engages in dialogue with Diamond and O'Connor's work on these units of material. Smith responds to the earlier work of his dialogue partners, material which still had a strongly historical approach to interpretation. He produces his own account of the textual limits of each confessional unit before contextualizing them within Jeremiah 11–20 and focusing on the divine speeches within the confessional sections, suggesting that overall the laments convey a developing relationship between prophet and people whereby Jeremiah is increasingly separate from his audience.

The later turn to rhetorical work, however, was less interested in historical issues and more in the literary mood and tone of prophetic messages, as the following chapters of this guide indicate. These interpretations of the prophetic book remain rooted in the contents of the Hebrew and Greek versions and their later editions, and share with historical analysts the interest in invasion and warfare. However, rather than seeking to deepen readers' understanding of these topics by historical contextualization, oriented to the past, they examine the metaphors of pain, terror and trauma by which the book constructs its message, in terms of how a modern audience could receive Jeremiah's message.

Experiences of warfare, bloodshed, rape and looting are part of our world, as shown in contemporary news programmes. For Europe, this reality was particularly painful with regard to two world wars and to instances of ethnic cleansing. Current European culture provides just one example of how regions have to find ways to rebuild trust and co-operation between indigenous groups after bitter division and competing acts of brutality have torn societies apart. Traumatic experience is a topic with which modern audiences can resonate, providing a communication bridge with a text which can appear remote from modern interests in its references to ancient Near Eastern politics and to battles fought and lost long ago.

Conflicts between cultures—imperial groups subordinating local groups: local groups regaining their independent voice—provide modern cultural theory with the topics of colonialism and post-colonialism. Using these cultural tools of analysis encourages readers to view an imperial culture both from its centre of power and from the excluded margins. This method of exegesis provides a further example of drawing on modern lived experience to provide a tool for critical analysis which can be applied historically, reading ancient texts within their own timeframe of imperial societies and which can also be of use in giving biblical texts the means of making a contribution to modern post-colonial debates.

## *Further Reading and References*

Barton, John
  1999    'Jeremiah in the Apocrypha and Pseudepigrapha', in Diamond *et al.* (1999): 396-19.
Bauer, Angela
  1999    'Dressed to Be Killed: Jeremiah 4:29-31 as an Example for the Functions of Female Imagery in Jeremiah', in Diamond *et al.* (1999): 293-305.
Bellis, Alice
  1999    'Poetic Structure and Intertextual Logic in Jeremiah 50', in Diamond *et al.* (1999): 179-99.
Brueggemann, W.
  1999    'The "Baruch Connection": Reflections on Jeremiah 43:1-7', in Diamond *et al.* (1999): 367-86.
Calloway, Mary
  1999    'Black Fire on White Fire: Historical |Context and Literary Subtext in Jeremiah 37–38', in Diamond *et al.* (1999): 171-78.
Carroll, R.
  1999    'The Book of J: Intertextuality and Ideological Criticism', in Diamond *et al.* (1999): 220-43.
Diamond, P.
  1987    *Confessions of Jeremiah in Context* (JSOTSup, 45; Sheffield: Sheffield Academic Press).
Diamond, P., K. O'Connor and L. Stulman (eds.)
  1999    *Troubling Jeremiah* (JSOTSup, 260; Sheffield: Sheffield Academic Press).
Domeris, William
  1999    'When Metaphor Becomes Myth: A Socio-linguistic Reading of Jeremiah', in Diamond *et al.* (1999): 244-62.
Froebel, K.
  1999    *Jeremiah's and Ezekiel's Sign Acts: Rhetorical Non-Verbal Communication* (Sheffield: Sheffield Academic Press).

Hill, John
    1999    'The Construction of Time in Jeremiah 25 (MT)', in Diamond *et al.* (1999): 146-60.
Holt, Else
    1999    'The Potent Word of God: Remarks on the Composition of Jeremiah 37–44', in Diamond *et al.* (1999): 161-70.
Job, J.
    2006    *Jeremiah's Kings: A Study of the Monarchy in Jeremiah* (Aldershot: Ashgate).
Kessler, Martin
    1999    'The Function of Chapter 25 and 50–51 in the Book of Jeremiah', in Diamond *et al.* (1999): 64-72.
Lee, Nancy
    1999    'Exposing buried subtext in Jeremiah and Lamentations: Going after Baal and…Abel', in Diamond *et al.* (1999): 87-122.
Lundbom, J.
    1975    *Jeremiah: A Study in Ancient Hebrew Rhetoric* (Atlanta, GA: Society of Biblical Literature).
O'Connor, Kathleen
    1999    'The Tears of God and Divine Character in Jeremiah 2–9', in Diamond *et al.* (1999): 387-403.
Olsen, Dennis
    1999    'Between the Tower of Unity and the Babel of Pluralism: Biblical Theology and Perdue's *The Collapse of History*', in Diamond *et al.* (1999): 350-58.
Overholt, T.
    1999    'What Shall We Do about Pluralism? A Response to Leo Perdue's *The Collapse of History*', in Diamond *et al.* (1999): 359-66.
Perdue, L.
    1999    'The Book of Jeremiah in Old Testament Theology', in Diamond *et al.* (1999): 320-38.
Person, Raymond, Jr
    1999    'A Rolling Corpus and Oral Tradition: A Not-so-Literate Solution to a Highly Literate Problem', in Diamond *et al.* (1999): 263-71.
Polk, T.
    1984    *The Prophetic Persona* (Sheffield: Sheffield Academic Press).
Saussure, Ferdinand de
    2013    *Course in General Linguistics* (London: Bloomsbury).
Skinner, John
    1930    *Prophecy and Religion: Studies in the Life of Jeremiah* (Cambridge: Cambridge University Press).
Smith, M.
    1990    *The Laments of Jeremiah and their Contexts: A Literary and Redactional Study of Jeremiah 11–20* (Atlanta, GA: Society of Biblical Literature).
Stulman, L.
    1999    'The Prose Sermons as Hermeneutical Guide to Jeremiah 1–25: The Deconstruction of Judah's Symbolic World', in Diamond *et al.* (1999): 34-65.
Wells, R.
    1999    'The Amplification of the Expectations of the Exiles in the MT Recension of Jeremiah', in Diamond *et al.* (1999): 272-92.

Chapter 6

TERROR, PAIN AND CHAOS:
THE RHETORICAL FOCUS ON JEREMIAH

Certain features of the book of Jeremiah strike any reader who pays close attention to the mood of the text. Apart from Jeremiah 30–31, the overwhelming tone of the material is one of disintegration of society and culture. As the geopolitics of the ancient Near East shifts to a new phase of Mesopotamian imperialism, with the rise of Assyria and then of Babylonia, small regional kingdoms face the threat of invasion and absorption into the larger territories to their north and east. In the Judahite kingdom power had resided in court and temple, with king and deity of one accord, presiding over local politics and ensuring success—an image provided by the account of Solomon's appeals for divine support on the occasion of the temple's consecration, in 1 Kings 8, for instance. But these joint authorities lose their power to shape Judah's religio-political identity once it has become a puppet state under foreign supremacy.

In Jeremiah's prose sermons key social symbols, such as those of temple and royal court, lose their power to keep the country safe (as has already been noted above with regard to Jeremiah 7): a reality which the prophet argues is due to false worship and elite complacency. For Jeremiah, it is the patron deity himself who is allowing such destruction with the result that the community experiences both the physical pain of warfare and the emotional disturbance of traumatic loss. This viewpoint is expressed, for example, in Jer. 11.17-18 where, through imagery of tents and shepherds as symbols for temple and kingship respectively, the text creates a landscape of vast desolation.

It is this socio-political reality which underlies the book and which is focalized in the rhetoric of characterization by the depiction of Jeremiah as the man of pain, as in the prophetic laments where the prophet speaks to God about his intolerable burden of pain and suffering and his reluctance to announce this message of pain to his fellow citizens, as in Jer. 16.11-18. Alongside the poetry of pain, the parallel prose narratives provide scenes which tell the story of fragmentation at the royal court with factions vying for royal support of their competing views on how the king should proceed with regard to Babylonian supremacy. The theme of lying prophets emerges as a motif which interprets factional politics from a Jeremianic perspective. In Jer. 23.10-12, for instance, competing councillors are attacked as lacking divine authority.

The previous chapter set out the framework of the scholarly move to rhetorical criticism, a form of exegesis which allows Jeremiah to be read synchronically, as a single work. This chapter explores the manner in which rhetorical studies have taken an interest in the symbolism of trauma and suffering which fills much of this biblical book. Historical criticism pointed to the separate nature of the layers of material which make up Jeremiah while rhetorical critics stress the over-arching mood of the prophetic book, but the sense of fragmentation provided by source criticism serves rhetorical issues well since it adds to the view that this biblical work is centred on themes of chaos and confusion. For both lines of interpretation, the so-called biographical parts of the book's contents add weight to the message which it wishes to communicate. Jeremiah as a human being, whether historical or literary, gathers into himself a nation's loss.

It is then the internal symbolic world of violence which is under consideration in rhetorical interpretation. From the angle of rhetorical exegesis, it is the literary world in its own right which is discussed, an approach which covers both the experiences of an original audience and those of modern readers: modern wartime experiences of traumatic disorder can be used to construct a suitable reading methodology, as well as making comparisons with modern survival literature (as referred to at the end of the previous chapter). In this context, the book of Jeremiah is viewed as a text which manages social disruption by employing robustly violent metaphors in order to provide a means of coming to terms with painful reality. Rhetorical studies acknowledge Jeremiah's historical context of the rise of new kingdoms in the ancient Near East but do not seek to match passages from Jeremiah with particular battles or defeats. Instead they look closely into the means by which the prophetic literature mediates a community's engagement with events beyond its control.

In order to illustrate how such rhetorical exploration can provide fresh understanding of a text's cultural relevance, particular attention will now be given to the work of Kathleen O'Connor and Louis Stulman, whose scholarly writings demonstrate the movement from an historical to a rhetorical method of reading Jeremiah. As such, these two scholars provide a bridge between historical and rhetorical explorations of the prophetic book; it is interesting to note in this regard how the focus on the speeches uttered by the character Jeremiah offered a basis for rhetorical interpretation.

In this regard, it is helpful to read Jer. 20.7-10 which paints a picture of deep anguish, as a man is caught between a hostile audience and an inner conviction of truth which has to be articulated. The immediacy of this first person material offers an opening into the ways in which readers are influenced by the books with which they engage. This was the case with Diamond and Polk, whose work was referred to in the previous chapter, as well as O'Connor. It can be suggested that the intimate, emotional tone of the lament units, for example, provided a rich field of study for rhetorical critics since this material highlights the emphasis on pain and terror which is found more widely in the book of Jeremiah. Meanwhile, the prose sermons provide a rational narrative which explains the sense of approaching doom which the prophet articulates.

In *The Confessions of Jeremiah* (1988), O'Connor gave a detailed exposition of each passage of Jeremiah's lament while also relating each one to the other texts in the sequence, with the aim of arriving at the overall purpose of the prophetic confessions. Her reading of the material led her to claim that the primary intention of the passages was to establish Jeremiah's authenticity as a true prophet and that this aim is carried through inside the text by using the *ribh* (legal indictment) formula in which the deity pursues a legal case against Judah, his covenant partner. Through the figure of the prophet, God gives evidence for his anger with Judah and justifies the disaster which will take place as occasioned by the infidelity of the people to their contract of allegiance with God. Jeremiah is thus characterized as prosecuting counsel on the deity's behalf.

O'Connor starts from an historical basis which seeks to place each passage in relation to specific events but concludes that it is impossible to provide solid answers to the historical issues of the date of each passage and the time of the book's final editing; instead she turns to the interior literary style and context of the final form of the book. She suggests that the lament units should be read in association with the prose sermons of the book; when this is done the literary function of the confessions emerges since, from this perspective, Israel's refusal to listen to God is focalized by Jeremiah's own struggles against the message of rejection and the people's rejection of him. The two literary styles of sermon and first person disclosure are mutually illuminative in terms of establishing the mood and tone of the book of Jeremiah as a whole.

O'Connor, whose original work on the confessions argued against the view that these passages provide evidence of an historical figure with a 'disordered personality', later returned to the theme of traumatic stress in her consideration of the deliberate literary usage of the suffering personal voice as a narrative weapon to stress the significance of Jeremiah's judgment on Judahite politics. In this later stage of her work she engaged not with the character of the historical prophet but with the characterization of that figure within the text. In a recent paper (2010), O'Connor focuses on the rhetorics of violence in Jeremiah, a discussion which she suggests engages with the frequently violent presentation of the deity in the Bible.

This profile of the divine, she notes, has not been an attractive subject for the students in her classes, but one against which they rebel.

But can one understand the role of the imagery of aggression in a more positive light? This question leads O'Connor to an examination of the rhetorical structure and function of an iconography of divine violence. Her answer to the modern audience's critique of the deity's character is that it is this threatening image which provides a literary strategy for setting out the message that a community can survive trauma and can pick up the pieces of social life to build a successful future. By setting the deity over warfare, making God the cause of war, social insecurity is controlled. Violence has its origins in divine anger with Judah's behaviour and such anger will pass away in due course. Thus a tool is offered for interpreting life's events which provides for survival of the community and its possible future renewal.

O'Connor's exegesis thus dialogues with the part played by pastoral activity in healing wounds after disaster and with the findings of modern trauma studies. She notes the component parts of traumatic experience— fragmented pieces of memory of disaster in the consciousness, incapacity to talk about experience, incapacity to feel emotion, the destruction of trust in God, world and people. Using this theoretical base, O'Connor argues for interpreting the work of Jeremiah as that of a theologian-poet who gives voice to the communal trauma, expressing powerfully the fears and doubts caused by lived experience which survivors cannot speak about in their own voice but which need to be brought to the forefront of consciousness, so that it is possible to come to terms with the past.

In times of attack by hostile forces, two common events are battlefield slaughter and the mistreatment of civilians, especially the raping of conquered women. O'Connor suggests that each of these themes is addressed by Jeremiah's poetry. She defines Jer. 4.5–6.30 as war poems and Jer. 13.20-27 as a rape poem which brings to speech the profound terror and harm of the Babylonian war. In the war poetry, actual battles are transferred to the cosmic realm and treated as mythic battles concerned with the 'foe from the north' and the Daughter of Zion. The text focuses the effects of many military acts through the violence done to a symbolic female scapegoat, imaging the deity as a sexual predator.

Even though this process results in the construction of a God who is violent and cruel, the link made between sin and judgment in the setting out of the war poems attempts to counter the even more threatening view that the deity is randomly cruel and wilfully violent: cosmic justice makes warfare necessary but also sets boundaries to it. This rhetorical move retains the possibility for the community which has been traumatized that it might once more find trust and safety in its religious beliefs. O'Connor refers in this context to the views of Walter Brueggemann (1998) where he talks about the motif of God and war as an open-ended, poetic reading of reality. She argues that the rhetorical strategy of the book of Jeremiah reflects the violence done to society but does not create it.

Whereas O'Connor has worked from Jeremiah's laments, Stulman has taken as his basis the prose sermons of Jeremiah. In his 1986 work on them, he took as his context the history of composition research of that time, especially the study of the Deuteronomic nature of source C (referring to Mowinckel's source theory). In his exegesis of the sermons, Stulman examined the Hebrew text in great detail in order to study diction and word use. He sought to discover whether the linguistic style of the material reveals an affiliation between the sermons and a wider Deuteronomic theology, which would impact on the potential dating of the sermons and on the broader topic of the order in which the contents of Jeremiah came into existence. This earlier study of the sermons provided a bridge for his later work which moves towards an examination of the rhetorical structure of the literary work, with an emphasis on the theme of chaos.

In his article of 1995 in *JSOT*, Stulman offers a rhetorical focus, using the model of insider/outsider as a way to investigate the book's primary literary symbols, noting that 'north', for example, is used as the code for peril while Babel symbolizes Zion's status with the deity. Babylon is the outsider, the foreign nation, while Zion stands for the insider community which the deity supports. Babylon attacks Judah, the outsider defeats the insider, thus rendering void the insider's beliefs in divine protection. In Jeremiah, though, Babylon functions as God's chosen tool for attacking Judah, thus acquiring insider status from its intimacy with the divine: now it is Judah which is pushed into an outsider position. In this rhetorical structure, the roles of insider and outsider are reversed, a move which puts the Judahite establishment into the role of divinely-ordained object of foreign attack. This is a counter-cultural move within the socio-political framework of the biblical book, one which disorientates the implied reader as much as the historical events pictured threatened assumed religious and civil values. The text operates a rhetorical strategy of dissonance and blurred borders, whose impact on the characterization of the deity is to turn God into a dangerous, volatile force, matched by the prophet's own untamed persona.

In *Order from Chaos* (1998), Stulman offers a full rhetorical treatment of Jeremiah's symbolic world. He starts from his own scholarly base in research on chaps. 1–25 of the book but is not here concerned with the origins of the separate sources of this section of Jeremiah. He looks instead to use an examination of the contents of source C to demonstrate how meaning is constructed across the whole book of Jeremiah. He reads chaps. 1–25 synchronically to identify their rhetorical structures and then applies this understanding to chaps. 26–52, also read synchronically. He argues that the text as a whole is shaped by the rhetorical structure of balancing hope against despair—a structure which gives full weight to the dysfunctional nature of war and defeat as the proper means of communicating a positive outcome for the community's future.

Central symbols such as king and temple remain valid in both phases of this process with their ongoing validity ensured only by the abandonment of their former manifestations. Only by turning away from the religious traditions, which have authorized royal ideology, and looking at the past afresh can society move beyond the collapse of central organs of government. In the old systems of society, secular and religious institutions worked to support the authority of an independent local elite but in order that religious belief can continue to function, and these symbols of cultural identity remain powerful, they have to be re-formulated for a province within a wider imperial kingdom. The symbols of ruler and cult remain important; there will be a new configuration of the Davidic ruler for instance, as noted in Jer. 30.8-9, where the yoke will be broken and foreign enslavement ended as 'David' is raised up in the shape of a new king. But these symbols must be detached from their older political realities and acquire new content in the post traumatic life of the community.

Stulman's work points to the social function of literature, linking his exploration of the textual world with the passages in the prose narratives where Jeremiah is shown writing scrolls, helped by Baruch—as in Jer. 36.4-7. Interpreting these passages, Stulman suggests that the scrolls represent another rhetorical symbol at work in the prophetic book. It is the 'scrolls', he suggests, which demonstrate the ways in which literature provides a bridging mechanism between past and future; by providing an imagined social world, literary works provide patterns for later communal re-structuring to take place—the written word becomes the symbol for a new vision of community.

O'Connor and Stulman, each in their own way, illustrate the chronological shift in Jeremiah studies from the project of explaining the meaning of the book by establishing its historical foundations to the search for its purpose as evidenced by its internal contents. Their work also demonstrates the turn to exploring the social function of written works more widely. As a book which counters the effects of social collapse affectively, by means of characterization and plot, Jeremiah functions as a reading site for audiences which have experienced terror or chaos. Exegesis of a literary work here engages the scholar with what is 'in front of' the book, with the readers' own social settings, from within which the reader engages with the content of the prophetic message. The needs of those who have been traumatized are matched with the provision of a book which delivers a symbolic traumascape. By engaging with this symbolic site, in Jeremiah's case a city on the verge of final collapse, readers can process their own histories of violent suffering.

The concept of using trauma theory as a vehicle for exploring the textual construction of Jeremiah has also been addressed by Mary Mills. Mills works with those aspects of trauma theory which have been engaged by cultural geographers, suggesting that Jeremiah be read as a traumascape. In her chapter on reading Jeremiah as a deathscape (2013), she explores the memorialization of space, via the work of the cultural geographer Karen Till. Till's work has engaged with the ways in which particular geographical spaces such as museums and memorials provide opportunities for processing communal traumas. Using Till's model, Mills suggests that the iconography of a withered landscape found in passages within Jeremiah 1–25 provides a suitable literary site for communal mourning over loss of land and the horrors of war. She draws on studies in the geography of violence as an entry into the concept of traumatization in the face of national danger. This opens into the nature of trauma studies, especially Maria Tumarkin's work on modern traumascapes, connected with twentieth-century war and ethnic cleansing.

As in O'Connor's recent work, Mills emphasizes the way in which traumatic stress renders a subject silent, bottling up the suffering produced by living through scenes of violent aggression which brought death and mutilation to many people engaged in these events. She suggests that the role of memory is central, since the survivor replays the scenes of violence interiorly. The ability to express these memories in an external forum is necessary if the trauma is to be processed and the individual or society to become capable of moving on from the past. A memorial site provides a legitimate space for mourning, a site which all can visit to perform acts of remembrance, a site which can ultimately bring together a fragmented community in a shared grief. Mills argues that texts can provide memory space in a similar manner to that provided by geographical sites. The imagery of the book of Jeremiah is an example of this provision, while the book of Lamentations demonstrates the nature of the mourning which can take place there. Whereas Jeremiah is a book which sets out the landscape of disaster in its oracles of judgment, the figure of widow Zion in Lamentations 1–2 focuses attention on human experience of disaster with the woman's lament at the loss of her children.

This chapter has so far dwelt on the worldviews of terror and chaos which poetic oracles and prose materials link with the invasion and defeat of the ancient kingdom of Judah. But as noted above, the book of Jeremiah contains material which situates such scenes of violence within the borders of other ancient city-states—the Oracles against the Nations, Jeremiah 46–51 in the Masoretic text of the book. Scholars working on the history of composition noted that the OANs form a common body of oracles found in prophetic books, especially the three major works of prophecy. This perspective permits scholars to work comparatively on such literary units as found in the canonical collection of the Hebrew Bible. In his 2004 study of the OANs, John Geyer makes a link between the use of lament and the mythology of divine warfare. He explores the rhetorical strategies of this oracular style, engaging in a schematic analysis of relevant passages, some of which are found in Jeremiah.

Geyer notes that the most characteristic grammatical form, used 13 times in Jeremiah, is the imperative command, followed by the Hebrew *ci* meaning for or because (22 times in Jeremiah). Thus, in Jer. 46.3-4 a series of commands set up the order of battle which is linked in v. 10 to the coming Day of the Lord and explained as the result of divine action in holding a sacrifice, a pattern repeated in vv. 13-21, where a series of commands leads eventually to the cause of these proclaimed events, which are named in v. 20 as a day of calamity. Geyer sees in these oracles a common style which also uses a set of common symbols comprised of water, north and mountain. In this rhetorical style, images of violence form part of the setting of communal lament, aligning everyday military acts with a cosmic warfare which provides a theophany, imaging a divine figure which comes with drawn sword to atone the land. Geyer considers that the basis for this rhetoric of divine appearance and slaughter is to be found in Exodus 12 with its depiction of a destroyer who will pass over the land seeking sacrificial atonement.

Geyer's study of Jeremiah's OANs offers a further version of rhetorical criticism, focused on the internal structure of oracles but seeking a common source for this rhetorical style from intertextual engagements between works of literature. Once defined, the lament form can be used in passages which name whichever states are currently viewed as problematic, using a commonly understood literary form consisting of superscription, destruction, lament, flight and theophany. Geyer looks for the origins of this style in the religious mythology which connects deity with holy war, an idea which can be viewed as sitting alongside O'Connor's argument that Jeremiah manages real trauma situations by creating a symbolic world of cosmic justice. In O'Connor's case, the aim of this approach is to explain troubling profiles of a deity while in Geyer's study the aim is to locate the pre-existing worldviews on which texts draw in their production of meaning.

This chapter has examined the turn to rhetorical analysis in detail with regard to the moods to be found in the book of Jeremiah. At the centre of these explorations are the experiences of real people in times of war, as illustrated and mediated by the figure of the prophet and the cast of the royal court. The book and the person of Jeremiah communicate a form of political theology which is intimately connected with bodies which bear the pain of loss. Citizens of the historical world are both subjects and objects of military commands; hence the concept of embodiment is a significant tool for assessing the rhetorical force of a literary work. It is to this aspect of rhetorical criticism which the next chapter turns.

However, before moving to consider the connections between the human form and rhetorical style, it is important to note that the book of Jeremiah shares a further common linguistic link with its companions in major written prophecy, Isaiah and Ezekiel. In the imagery of earth mourning, Katherine Hayes (2002) finds passages which treat the earth as an embodied persona. In Jeremiah such materials are present in chaps. 4, 12 and 23. They have as a common theme the idea of land shaking, of cosmic upheaval and of desolation and chaos. In these literary scenes, the earth is a created form which is in relation with human beings, the wicked, and with the deity. What human beings do impacts directly on the earth. The earth mourns as it suffers stripping, pollution and de-creation—all of them physical events.

Hayes argues that Jer. 12.7-13 in particular demonstrates an iconography of earth as a person since it responds to God's wishes while the people of Judah remain hostile and indifferent to the deity. The earth's suffering is the reflection of the curse imposed on it as a result of evil human activity, thus making it into a body wherein mourning is expressed in physical terms. The earth carries bodily the pain of the disrupted relations between deity and human inhabitants. Thus the phrase 'the earth mourns' provides a metaphor for the effects of warfare in ravaging the land as well as a symbol for the cosmic dysfunctionality, the return to chaos, which human violence shares with a reciprocating divine aggression.

In this rhetorical construction, an important move is made by which the physical environment takes on the role of messenger and mediator, becoming a prophetic force in its own self. It is driven outside its intended role within the wider cosmic plan for harmonious relationships between creator, created habitat and created species. Harmony in the cosmos holds all life together, giving the cosmic body an ordered stable profile. The cosmic body has its own shape, with its external borders. These borders are transgressed as noted in Jer. 4.23-26 where the cosmos is driven beyond its proper shape, becoming formless as mountains quake and fertile land turns to desert. It is the balance between ordered bodily function and activity which is in excess of settled limits which form the basis for examining the rhetorical construction of the divine and prophetic bodies in Jeremiah, as will be demonstrated in the next chapter.

*Further Reading and References*

Brueggemann, W.
  1998    *A Commentary on Jeremiah: Exile and Homecoming* (Grand Rapids, MI: Eerdmans).
Diamond, P. (ed.)
  1999    *Troubling Jeremiah* (London: T. & T. Clark International).
Geyer, J.
  2004    *Mythology and Lament: Studies in the Oracles about the Nations* (Aldershot: Ashgate).

Hayes, K.
2002    *'The Earth Mourns': Prophetic Metaphor and Oral Aesthetic* (Atlanta, GA: Society of Biblical Literature).

Mills, M.
2013    *Urban Imagination in Biblical Prophecy* (London: T. & T. Clark International).

O'Connor, K.
1988    *The Confessions of Jeremiah: Their Interpretation and Role in Chapters 1–25* (Atlanta, GA: Society of Biblical Literature).
2010    'Reclaiming Jeremiah's Violence', in C. Franke and J. O'Brien (eds.), *Aesthetics of Violence in the Prophets* (London: T. & T. Clark International), pp. 37-49.

Stulman, L.
1986    *The Prose Sermons of the Book of Jeremiah* (Atlanta, GA: Society of Biblical Literature).
1995    'Insiders and Outsiders in the Book of Jeremiah: Shifts in Symbolic Arrangements', *JSOT* 66: 65-85.
1998    *Order from Chaos* (Sheffield: Sheffield Academic Press).

Till, Karen
2005    *The New Berlin: Memory, Politics, Place* (Minneapolis: University of Minnesota Press).

Tumarkin, Maria
2005    *Traumascapes* (Melbourne: University of Melbourne Press).

Chapter 7

## BODIES, SPACE AND EXCESS AS CONCEPTUAL
## TOOLS FOR READING JEREMIAH

As Chapters 5 and 6 have demonstrated, rhetorical criticism engages the reader with the narrative space of a literary text; it promotes close attention to the manner in which words and phrases are used within the boundaries of a piece of literature and to the wider shaping of contents by metaphor and symbol. Although this task is initially one of internal textual analysis, it broadens out into investigation of the contexts in which different audiences read the same book, since different readers take up the range of symbolic meaning which a metaphor contains in ways specific to their cultural context. Hence the close reading of texts which engagement in rhetorical studies requires is balanced by the need to attend to the reading site occupied by specific audiences. In both activities the underlying focus is on space, the narrative space of words and phrases and the social space of the reader's culture, from within which a reader encounters a literary work.

In this chapter, attention is given to a number of contemporary reading sites—that is, cultural locations of communities of readers—which influence interpretation of the book of Jeremiah. Some of these emerge from modern literary criticism while others draw on the interests of specific audiences, as in feminist and postcolonial discourse: topics which will be addressed in detail in the rest of this chapter. Common to these varied approaches to reading Jeremiah is the concept of embodiment—a perspective which aims to break down the dualism between mind and body. When a reader engages with a text it is as a fully human person, physically situated in time and place that s/he does so, bringing to bear on the act of reading concerns which belong with that material state. Physical embodiment in turn generates bodily concepts which function as a powerful metaphorical tool in literature, as has already been noted in the previous chapter.

Since human beings engage in intellectual activity as fully embodied individuals, it is likely that the experience of material existence will inform the paradigms they devise in order to communicate symbolically. The geographer Yi-Fu Tuan (1977), for instance, noted that the elemental symbolism for measuring wider spaces comes from the nature of bodily life, with the head, arms and legs being aligned with points of the compass. Overall, then, bodies and embodiment are topics which produce metaphoric language for establishing social boundaries and demarcating groups from each other. In this chapter, interpretations of the book of Jeremiah which emerge from reading the book via spatial and social locations will be explored.

As already noted in previous chapters, there is a particular focus on the individual figure of the prophet in Jeremiah and this provides a point of access for readings which focus on the experience of being an embodied individual. The book's use of a single character to focalize a verdict on religio-political culture can be aligned with insights concerning embodiment drawn from wider critical theory. Contemporary critical readings reflect on the issues of what constitutes a body, what kinds of bodies there are, and where the border between bodies lies. These wider issues in contemporary theory can be adapted by scholars to provide a fresh perspective on biblical works.

For example, a key marker for the creation of social norms is the preferred body. Such a body is the type of physical form which is idealized by a given society and is used to define the social stereotypes which community members then strive to attain. In this regard, Judith Butler (1993) has pointed to the stereotyping of bodies via the social acts which they perform, such as work in the public sphere or work within a family home. Bodily forms which do not fit into preferred categories are often labelled dysfunctional or deformed, as argued for instance in the work of sociologist Rosemarie Thomson (1997) where she explores the concept of Extraordinary Bodies, bodies which do not fit a given social standard and so become symbols of the deviant and disordered world which threatens social cohesion. One such symbol is the [dis]abled body and Mary Mills (2007) uses this motif to create a reading lens for the profile of Jeremiah generated by the confessional material in this prophetic book.

Mills labels this usage prophetic pathos, understanding pathos here to be constituted by the impact on Jeremiah's embodied stance as mediator between God and people, a stance composite of pain and moral indignation which impacts upon his material existence. Jeremiah's mediator position aligns his body as a site of personal deterioration with the social collapse of his community, which God has come to regard as liminal, under threat of divine erasure. The prophetic body is affected physiologically by the occupation of this social space, forced by the deity to disown loyalty to his fellow citizens since Jeremiah must pronounce their destruction, yet seemingly abandoned by God to conspiratorial violence and rejection by his audience (as noted in Chapter 6 above). In the confessions, the reader overhears the desperate petitions and laments made by Jeremiah to his God and the atmosphere of this material turns increasingly claustrophobic and paranoid.

It is Jeremiah's mental health which is deformed here, Mills argues, with the result that he can be characterized as a disabled body, crippled by his task of representing the state of chaos found outside ordered society. The deformed persona of the prophet is held up by the narrator of the prose stories as a true mirror of Judahite society. The disorder within the prophet's emotions embodies his message that the normative institutions of proper society, kingship and temple, are about to be totally dismembered. Jeremiah is presented as at the centre of court life in the prose narratives, yet his vocation is to undo the bonds which tie that community together.

The text plays on the interchanging roles of insider and outsider, a theme noted above with regard to the work of Stulman and which challenges the readers of the prophetic book in relation to their understanding of the proper form of prophetic embodiment. Mills suggests that Jeremiah's disabled body provides a model for the reader to side with the moral pathos of the emotionally crippled individual and challenges the dismissal of the possibility that disabled bodies can contribute anything worthwhile to mainstream social values. By standing in excess of communal norms, the prophetic body signals what is grotesque—confusion, loss of identity, failed relationships. In this manner, Jeremiah's chaotic life signals the deregulation of familiar patterns of order, moving readers into the field of ambiguity.

In the literary profile of a figure of pathos, Jeremiah's body occupies a space which is parallel to that occupied by female bodies according to feminist interpretations of the biblical book. Steed Vernyl Davidson (2013), writing on the gendered construction of sacred space in Jeremiah, dwells on the 'out-of-placeness' of female figures in this book. He notes how chap. 7 gives women's cultic rituals to honour the Queen of Heaven as a central example of bad worship which angers God. Women's rituals take place on the streets and so are already excluded from the central worship site; the streets function as an illicit cultic site, corrupted by the worship of alien deities. Steed notes that it is specifically women who stand here for the evil which the population engages in.

The topic of female cultic activity arises again in Jeremiah 44 when the refugee group is in Egypt. According to Steed, the reference to the worship of the Queen of Heaven here is more ambiguous. Jeremiah denounces it and yet seems to tell the women that they can continue these rites if they wish. The text of vv. 16-19 can be read as giving the women subjective voice as they claim that all was well when their cults went on as normal in the past. Steed suggests that although the text is ambivalent it can be argued that there is a marginal female space constructed by the speech of the women in Egypt, a site which subverts the primacy of the temple space at Jerusalem as the only sacred space available to Judahites. Steed concludes that the literary motif of an exilic group (itself located outside the normal boundaries of society) provides a rhetorical refuge-space for those on the periphery of standard community structures.

Both Mills and Davidson explore how Jeremiah can be read to offer fresh cultural meaning in ways which emphasize the function of a prophet to be on the margins of society in some way, while also acting as the voice of truth in that community. The commentary series 'Feminist Companion to the Bible' also provides a feminist critique of biblical books and in the volume on Prophets and Daniel (2nd series, 2001), Judith Hadley also discusses the theme of the worship of the Queen of Heaven in chaps. 7 and 44 of Jeremiah. While it is clear in Jeremiah 7 that women take the lead in false worship, Hadley considers Jeremiah 44 to be more nuanced, as against the views of O'Connor who sees the same message of women's deviance in both chapters. She points out that the immediate response to the women's claim for the empowerment coming from their rituals is that they can go ahead and it is only in a subsequent section of this scene that the prophet issues a message of doom, referring to an event in the distant future. Once again, space is made for validating the experiences of a marginal group in the community.

From that biblical opening, Hadley presses into consideration of the presence of the 'goddess' in monotheistic, masculine text as a separate divinity. The work of Teresa Ellis (2009) takes this idea further by investigating the actions which Jeremiah 7 states have angered YHWH. Although Jeremiah condemns women's ritual, the supporters of the Queen of Heaven say that it is not their acts which have caused disaster but those actions of the kings of Judah which were intended to suppress the female cult. Could we then construct from this dialogue a scenario in which the Queen of Heaven is intimately associated with the God of Israel? Or, as Hadley suggests, since all Judahite worship post exile becomes monotheistic, worship of alternative divinities is subsumed into this belief. Ellis' paper moves from materially embodied but marginalized citizens to the question of divine embodiment and the search for feminine divinity within the over-arching religious tradition. Such a divine presence could be used as a role model to underline the place of women in human affairs.

Alongside Hadley's commentary on chap. 44 of Jeremiah, Mary Shields, in the same volume, discusses Jer. 3.1-44 under the title of the circumcision of the prostitute. Shields begins from the basic stance that pre-exilic texts are generally hostile to the female gender, using gendered language to depict what is subversive and deviant in social activity. In Jeremiah 3, the text moves from accusation to promise, a move mirrored by the shift from female imagery to male images. Jeremiah 2, which addresses a male audience as 'you plural', describes this group as having acted as prostitutes in the high places while Jer. 3.1 which is also addressed to males uses the image of female adultery leading to divorce as the woman passes to the space of another male; in this situation for the first male to seek to have his wife back would be corrupt. This imagery of adultery and divorce is woven into description of the land, which has been corrupted by the action of the (male) addressees who have prostituted themselves in idolatrous worship. In the second part of the chapter, God promises restoration of relations, taking the part of the husband in a relationship, promising caring king-shepherds as future rulers. In v. 23 the cult on the high hills is foresworn.

Shields interprets this material as creating meaning based on gendered imagery which continually undermines women's subjective experience. The female becomes an object which focalizes male discourse, illuminating by negative contrast the proper pattern of male behaviour. Women's bodies operate on the threshold between order and chaos and as such they provide regulatory principles while themselves drifting towards the chaos outside social order. They are both a non-porous border shutting off threats and a porous surface which can absorb alien reality. Shields reflects on this use of language from the angle of a modern set of readers, embedded in their own cultural issues. Does such ancient textual usage remain a valid object for study or does receiving and studying this material affect the relationship between women as subjects and the wider culture in our own day? Does it continue to undermine women-space even now?

In her monograph on Jer. 3.1–4.4 (2004), Shields expands her reading method to the field of Bakhtinian intertextuality, the interaction of multiple voices. She argues that metaphor is used in Jeremiah 3 as a narrative rhetorical strategy and attaches to that view the suggestion that it is gender which constructs the metaphor in this passage. The textual account of the past, present and future of the relations between God and people is governed by such gendered metaphor in which circumcision of the body plays a key part. The profile of Israel is shaped by the circumscribing of female behaviour, denoted in sexual terms. Male behaviour is prescribed as the antidote to the damage caused by deviant female activity. Shields builds, in this volume, on earlier work on the use of female sexual imagery in prophecy, identified by Phyllis Bird and Claudia Camp.

Feminist readings of Jeremiah thus engage in understanding the ancient text through the lens of the social power relations of the present time. They focus on the metaphorical use which texts make of the imagery of the female body with regard to sexual activity and social norms. Renita Weems (1995), for instance, points out that Jeremiah shaped his message around cultural contempt for immodest women, developing this with regard to the marriage metaphor—an image which emerged from the ancient legal practice of viewing women as the property of their husbands. Husbands had the authority to enforce their will on their wives. The use of the metaphor in Jeremiah highlights even further the emotionally charged mood of the book with its profile of urgency, agitation, desperation and frustration.

In Jeremiah, loose female behaviour is viewed as self-consciously per-formed, the women know what they are doing. This leads the narrator to the judgment that these women's skirts will be lifted over their heads; this image is shockingly brutal, engaging not only shame but the idea of rape. Moreover, it is the deity who not only permits but endorses this male vio-lence. The reading site of women's experience questions the validity of such a scene as an acceptable piece of religious teaching. Although Weems goes on to note how Jeremiah 30–31 treats female imagery in a positive light as a metaphor for restoration of land rights to the community, this does not remove the trace of permissible violence against female subjects. The res-toration of virgin Israel in Jer. 31.4, together with a tender care for mothers (v. 8) does not justify the use of the motif in Jer. 5.10-14 where the daughter of Zion is given over to murderers.

An essential issue in the study of embodiment as expressive of contests over social identity is the balance between what is normative and what is excessive—what stands outside the norm, what exceeds standard cultural borders, as explained above. The literary genres which have been used to explore this balance include those of Horror and the Grotesque. Amy Kalmanofsky (2008) used the work of Noel Carroll on the Horror genre to examine aspects of the rhetorical structure of Jeremiah. She suggests that horrible encounters provoke fear and disgust and lead to the construc-tion of monsters. One typical context for this process is found in warfare, which produces both physical and emotional terror. Jeremiah contains a great many scenes of military violence; in Jer. 6.24, for instance, the fear of warriors facing a vast enemy force is linked with women's birth-pangs, the strength of soldiers undermined by a 'womanly' pain.

Kalmanofsky argues that this material creates its own monster—the deity. God is the monster because the deity is the single worst threat to the stability of Judah. The divine monster is an ambivalent figure since bibli-cal monsters represent the chaotic forces defeated at creation but still threat-ening order. God is set over against such figures but is drawn into their midst as the one who causes warfare. In Jer. 19.10-11 the image of God the Waster, the cannibal, appears since as God's monstrous body the enemy from the north sweeps down to consume Judah (Jer. 19.7). A second type of monstrous reality is created by this divine action as the devastated vic-tims are portrayed as themselves monsters, eating the flesh of their children in Jer. 1.19.

In this context, Kalmanofsky refers to Julia Kristeva's theory of the abject body to critique the use of images of the corrupted body with its wounds, the decaying matter of corpses. The aim of this rhetorical usage in Jeremiah is not to shock for its own sake but to serve the serious purpose of main-taining social order. God the Destroyer and Israel the Destroyed are two faces of the same iconography: read together they point to divine control of events, even of traumatic and totally threatening events. They function to regulate a hope in the survival of the community of Judah—a topic already examined in Chapter 6 above.

In these studies of the rhetorical structure of the book of Jeremiah from the vantage point of embodiment, the perspective of the reader shifts both from the historical author and the literary stylistics to the ideological interests which the book pursues and the language by which it does so. That which is marginal to the main thrust of the text becomes a central focus for study. The use of gendered language to denounce male behaviour in effect marginalizes women, while the focus on multiple corpses and cannibalism produces scenes which violate human decency. Critics of this literary iconography aim to reverse the direction of reader's gaze, requiring the reader to engage with the marginalized other in her own right.

The explorations of embodiment conducted in this chapter have so far demonstrated that the ideological use of the human body and of gender has diverse styles which nevertheless share a common concern with identifying the particular location of the site from which the reader engages with the biblical material since they variously claim that it is from this position in front of the text that meaning is made. It is important to consider the impact of ideological symbolism in linking ancient texts with modern theoretical frameworks. Gender study uses the location of the modern audience of Jeremiah as a key tool for exegesis, requiring the reader to reflect on what a text does to the mind-set of the person who engages with it. Meanwhile, Kalmanofsky's research pursues a literary-critical perspective on embodiment as social symbol, engaging with the work of female theorists whose work follows the psychological framework set out by Jacques Lacan.

So far, this chapter has engaged in some detail with reading from a womanist lens but now a further example of the importance of embodied readership in the development of meaning will be added. This second example of the rhetorical style under investigation with regard to Jeremiah is found in the area of postcolonial research. Post-colonialism has a wider existence than as an interpretive tool for biblical studies, being an area of critical theory in its own right, connected with the view that texts mirror the ideologies of the politically powerful societies from which they emerge. The literary motifs of plot, characterization, and time and place setting are defined according to the viewpoints of the cultural centre of a given society.

An oft-quoted literary example of this reality is the way in which characterization of the first wife of Mr Rochester in *Jane Eyre* as deviant and monstrous plays upon the fact that she comes from outside normal English society and is the embodiment of the colonial subject, the alien culture of the colonies held by the British Empire in the nineteenth century. Having this profile, she cannot be the proper wife for an English landowner and her death with its concomitant damage to the hero and his property features as the proof of the bad choices made in the hero's youth. Postcolonial enquiry names the traces of imperialism found in texts and addresses the ways in which a colonial culture manages its relations with a dominant, foreign worldview through producing its own literature.

Davidson (2011) applies the reading stance of post-colonialism to commenting on the way in which the book of Jeremiah constructs meaning. This monograph takes seriously the book's stated context of exilic culture and aligns this with modern treatments of the ways in which local communities are dominated by global powers but still resist total immersion in imperial concerns. Davidson suggests that Jeremiah can be read through that lens, as a book of subtle resistance to Babylonian takeover, citing as evidence ideas from the critical theorists Tuan, Doreen Massey and R.S. Sugirtharajah, whose books relate to the fields of cultural geography and biblical studies. Like other reading strategies, this method also stresses the high profile given to the life and times of the prophet in the book of Jeremiah; Davidson pays tribute to earlier works of Jeremiah scholarship which examined the prophetic profile, including those of Diamond and Polk discussed in Chapter 6 above.

Davidson engages with postcolonial theorists such as Gayatri Spivak and Homi Bhabha to shape his examination of three passages from the prose material of Jeremiah—chaps. 29, 32 and 40. The study of Jeremiah 32 focuses on Jeremiah's purchase of land in the district of Anathoth as a metaphor of resistance to loss of ancestral territory. If the prophet can validly purchase a plot of land and own it then the community can retain its hopes for land restoration. Land constitutes an identity symbol drawn from the past of the people and the link with the past re-inscribes traditional values into a text which is imperially-angled in its message of acceptance of Babylonian supremacy. For Davidson, Jeremiah 40 produces a second symbol of resistance connected with the prophet: he is silent in the face of apparent marginalization in the narrative but his silence is a form of 'speaking back' to the overlord. When someone refuses to respond verbally to events beyond their control they perform an act of quiet resistance to the conversation whose scope is determined by powerful interests.

Thirdly, there is the matter of the letter written by Jeremiah in chap. 29. The experience of exiles generally is one of being 'away from home', an event which necessitates communication by written form. In these letters from exile, the writer often re-balances cultural identity, drawing from past and present cultural models, creating a hybrid identity. Jeremiah's letter sets out ground rules for the exiles. This material can be read 'from above' as endorsing the right of rulers to take people from their homes and lands since it accepts the new status quo. At the same time, it can be read 'from below' as a further example of hidden resistance. Davidson suggests that in telling the exiles to build solid houses and to ensure the continuity of their families Jeremiah resists the decay of traditional culture and cultural absorption into the new host society.

While nationalism can no longer provide a reliable focus for cultural continuity, religious praxis offers a substitute tool for promotion of social cohesion, Davidson suggests. The theology of the Covenant relationship between God and society provides a point of unity between history and lifestyle, balancing the theme of Exile with that of Exodus. The Israelites did not win freedom from Egypt by their own efforts but were liberated by a deity into 'slavery' to his service. In the times of kings, this reality was embedded in society by palace and temple systems of governance; now, in exile, the same identity is to be carried by the domestic organization of family life. According to this interpretation, in encouraging the exiles in their religion Jeremiah is quietly undermining the tendency of victorious regimes to destroy the individual identities of subject peoples.

A volume which brings together postcolonial and feminist perspectives on meaning in Jeremiah is the recent collection of papers made by Christl Maier and Carolyn Sharp (2013). The book pulls together materials presented at a series of conferences and research gatherings including the Reading/Writing Jeremiah unit of the Society of Biblical Literature's San Francisco meeting in 2011. In their introduction to the volume, the editors look back over 30 years of Jeremiah scholarship, a period which has seen the continued use of historical-critical approaches as well as the rise of postmodern methodologies. They advocate the need for commentators on Jeremiah to be self-aware with regard to the merits and messages of a range of reading styles while pointing out that both feminist and postcolonial perspectives are concerned with analyses of power relations within ancient texts and within the schools of textual interpretation.

They note that the papers in their volume share an interest in deconstructionist and audience-related modes of interpretation in which embodiment is viewed as the 'real' context of meaning. In her paper, Sharp notes with regard to her own academic work that her earlier work took for granted the scholarly context of a largely male profile among researchers and made use of historical criticism without reflecting on the significance of these underlying realities. Even so, her book on ideology in Jeremiah argued for the existence of multiple geographic settings within which Jeremiah traditions arose and were nurtured, thus engaging with the topics of diversity and location as worthy of attention in their own right. Both interpretive strands concern themselves with that which is 'other' and how the other is a source of meaning for a group which defines itself as 'us'. The scholarly contributions explore how the gap between the familiar and the strange is exploited in the book of Jeremiah in the interests of deconstructing an elite worldview.

Hence Yosefa Raz discusses how Jeremiah's call narrative breaks the lineage between father/son, modelling the fragility of social relations, while Juliana Claassens examines the anti-women stance of the metaphor of women in labour used nine times in Jeremiah to demonstrate male weakness. She suggests that the focus on pain in childbirth uses a woman's voice for male ends. The focus on pain creates a trauma site which is not only that of Judah but of the 'other' nations, as the metaphor is used in the OANs in Jeremiah. Claassens asks whether prophetic eloquence concerning social collapse even of the foreign nations may show an empathy with those communities which are subjected to imperial control. Davidson meanwhile uses Bhabha's theories to examine an exoticizing of the other as applied to the Rechabites in Jeremiah 35. In this approach the other is both colonialized as racially and sexually different, and at the same time desired.

Stulman's contribution extends analytical scrutiny of ancient text to examination also of the scholarly commentary. He argues that the image of Jeremiah's memoir as fragmentary and disunited describes also the genre of the scholarly commentary. Both literary styles are self-referential activities in which units of meaning accumulate in a non-strucured manner so allowing for the complexity of meaning as this emerges from lived experience. This paper responds to the views expressed in the editorial introduction to the volume which points out that it is not only ancient literature which is driven by ideological interests, scholars also are shaped by the world in which they live and embed the interests of that world in their approach to textual interpretation. Scholars need to be self–aware of their own reading sites and cultural preconceptions.

This chapter has explored recent movements of rhetorical enquiry into Jeremiah which move from a focus on the internal structures of literary works as the source of meaning to the view that meaning is produced by readers and that different audiences provide different interpretations. Whereas historical-critical scholarship seeks the single truth of a text's meaning insofar as this is derived from its historical origins and authorial intention, the turn to ideological criticism has led to the promotion of texts as having many meanings, as many as those of the individual readers of the work. The text as a piece of literature provides a meeting point between these two exegetical approaches since it is the book's words and phrases that provide the evidence for discussions about meaning.

Whereas these materials are the data for answering the question of historical criticism, who wrote this book and why, for contextual criticism the same material provides the data for the question, what influence does this book have on a reader and how does the profile of the reader shape the meaning which is perceived within a given book. The sharp edges of real life thus refuse to be flattened into a tidy, single meaning. The attention to rhetorical and contextual approaches to exegesis provided in this

chapter, and the previous one, demonstrates how focusing on ancient literature in terms of its layers of composition gives way to identifying first
a suitable strand of modern cultural theory which is examined for its own
concerns before being used to produce a reading lens for the investigation
of the book of Jeremiah.

But in the attention given to diversity of interpretive style and the social
production of biblical works has the essential place of religion been over-
looked? Is it still possible to speak of the theological meaning of Jeremiah?
In response to the emphasis laid on the importance of variety and difference
in interpreting the book of Jeremiah in the main papers of Maier and Sharp's
edited book, Brueggemann suggests that there is a valid model of disorien-
tation in what the essayists are doing, challenging the reasonableness of the
model of monolithic intellectual worldview derived from the views of the
philosopher Rene Descartes.

At the same time, Brueggemann turns the critique of a falsely unitive
approach back on the post-modern school of thought, challenging the
reductionism of readings which run together the character of the deity with
the ideologies of a dominant political group. Brueggemann's essay offers a
point of contact between diversity and theology in his view that the stress on
trauma studies provides a means of meeting the problems of simplification
of meaning in Jeremiah since they focus on exploring theological meaning
but from the angle of randomness. It is the case that rhetorical analysis with
its synchronic approach to the book of Jeremiah allows for investigation of
the religious messages of the text as a whole.

Brueggemann is himself a major scholar in the field of biblical theology, one who accepts the broad outlines of history of composition
research while drawing on rhetorical examination of the book of Jeremiah
as a means of accessing its teachings on the nature of the deity and of
human behaviour. His contributions to Jeremiah scholarship extend from
the mid-twentieth century to the present day, including commentaries and
critiques of the book of Jeremiah as well as an overall treatment of the
theology of the Old Testament. In his work, Brueggemann is constantly
aware of the need to communicate with the worldview and socio-political
context of modern-day communities of faith. The next chapter turns to
these questions about God and humanity as they are illustrated by the contents of Jeremiah, bringing together the parallel topics of theology, story
and history.

### Further Reading and References

Bird, Phyllis
    1989   "'To Play the Harlot": An Inquiry into an Old Testament Metaphor', in Peggy
           Day (ed.), *Gender and Difference in Ancient Israel* (Minneapolis: Fortress
           Press) 75-94.

Brenner, A. (ed.),
2001    *Prophets and Daniel* (Feminist Companion to the Bible, Second Series; London: Continuum).
Brueggemann, Walter
2013    'A Response by Walter Brueggemann', in Maier and Sharp (2013): 224-33.
Butler, J.
1993    *Bodies That Matter: On the Discursive Limits of 'Sex'* (London: Routledge).
Camp, Claudia
1999    'What's So Strange about the Strange Woman', in David Jobling, Peggy Day and Gerald Sheppard (eds.), *The Bible and the Politics of Exegesis* (Cleveland: Pilgrim Press) 17-31.
Claassens, Juliana
2013    'Like a Woman in Labour…', in Maier and Sharp (2013): 117-32.
Davidson, S.V.
2011    *Empire and Exile: Postcolonial Readings of the Book of Jeremiah* (London: Bloomsbury).
2013    'Every Green Tree and the Streets of Jerusalem: Counter Constructions of Gendered Sacred Space', in Mark George (ed.), *Constructions of Space*, IV (London: Bloomsbury) 111-31.
2013    'Exoticizing the Other…', in Maier and Sharp (2013): 189-207.
Ellis, T.
2009    'Jeremiah 44: What if the Queen of Heaven is YHWH?', *JSOT* 33: 465-88.
Hadley, J.
2001    'The Queen of Heaven—Who is She?', in Brenner (2001): 30-53.
Kalmanofsky, A.
2008    *Terror All Around: Horrors, Monsters and Theology in the Book of Jeremiah* (London: T. & T. Clark International).
Maier, C., and C. Sharp (eds.)
2013    *Prophecy and Power: Jeremiah in Feminist and Postcolonial Perspective* (New York/London: Bloomsbury).
Massey, Doreen
2005    *For Space* (Sage Thousand Oaks California).
Mills, M.
2007    *Alterity, Pain and Suffering in Isaiah, Jeremiah and Ezekiel* (London: T. & T. Clark International).
Raz, Yosefa
2013    'Jeremiah 'before the Womb', in Maier and Sharp (2013): 86-100.
Sharp, C.
2003    *Prophecy and Ideology in Jeremiah* (London: T. & T. Clark International).
Shields, M.
2004    *Circumcision of the Prostitute: Gender, Sexuality and the Call to Repentance in Jeremiah 3:1-44* (Sheffield: Sheffield Academic Press).
Shields, M.
2009    'Circumcision of the Prostitute: Gender, Sexuality and the Call to Repentance in Jeremiah 3:1-44', in Brenner (2001): 121-34.
Spivak, Gayatri
2006    *In Other Worlds: Essays in Cultural Politics* (London: Routledge).
Stulman, Louis
2013    'Reflections on Writing/Reading War and Hegemony in Jeremiah and Contemporary US Foreign Policy', in Maier and Sharp (2013): 57-71.

Sugirtharajah, R.S.
    2011    *Postcolonial Reconfigurations: An alternative way of reading the Bible and doing theology* (London: SCM Press).
Thomson, R.
    1997    *Extraordinary Bodies: Figuring Physical Disability in American Culture and Literature* (New York: Columbia University Press).
Tuan, Y.-F.
    1997    *Space and Place: The Perspective of Experience* (Minneapolis: University of Minnesota Press).
Weems, R.
    1995    *Battered Love: Marriage, Sex and Violence in the Hebrew Prophets* (Minneapolis: Fortress Press).

Chapter 8

JEREMIAH: THEOLOGY, STORY, HISTORY

The inclusion of Jeremiah in the canonical collection of the Bible points to the fact that its identity is ultimately to be found in its dealings with the nature of divine activity within the world of human affairs. In this context, it is proper to speak of the book as a theological work. A theological emphasis is centred neither on the cultural causes of a book's production nor on the ideological impact of the ancient book on readership but rather on the religious dimensions of Jeremiah—its approach to the character and work of the deity and the relations between God and the created world. As noted at the end of the previous chapter, a tension can be identified between the tendency for theological readings to look for a single unitive meaning in the book and the fact that the book of Jeremiah is composed of individual units of text which do not always dovetail easily with each other.

Historical criticism concerned itself with the history of composition, an approach which separated out the individual subunits of material. Yet all these units of text involve the same God, the patron deity of Judah, who is described as being in charge not only of Judah but of the ancient Near East. The shaping of Jeremiah's task in Jeremiah 1 and 45, to pull down and build up cities and kingdoms, and the opening of Jeremiah 46 where he is defined as prophet to the nations imply that the prophet is the mouthpiece of a deity whose power shapes the destinies of the region, from Egypt in the south to Babylon in the north. It is this evidence which lies behind Duhm's argument that a major message of the books of written prophecy is ethical monotheism—a theological perspective which argues that the belief that there is only one God, who is a universal figure, is aligned with a strongly ethical code of behaviour.

Any worship practice which does not address itself to the universal deity is false and corrupt and worship of this God requires of worshippers that they behave justly towards their fellow human beings, as indicated in the Sinaitic code in the book of Exodus and Deuteronomy and reflected in the preaching of Jeremiah. The oracles of Jeremiah 1–25, which describe the coming invasions as divinely-led, follow the model of sin and punishment. These events are caused by failure on the part of the elite class to provide true leadership, especially in its practice of polytheistic worship and hence the disasters are also justified and explicable as divine acts of judgment against Judah. This interpretation of the theology of prophecy takes a plain reading of the text as its foundation, following the attitude towards social guilt and divine anger at human failure to keep the terms of the covenant which is clearly present in the final text of Jeremiah. The corollary of this teaching is that the deity emerges as a harsh figure who demands retribution for lack of loyalty on the part of his human subjects. It is this avenging cosmic force whose profile is critiqued by rhetorical criticism, as shown in Chapter 7 above.

As has been shown above, the Jeremiah passages which describe the harsh political events as divine justice can be interrogated in terms of their rhetoric of terror; they can be treated with caution for their creation of a symbolic divine monster. The divine characterization in Jeremiah deals with harsh and cruel events, with the constant threat of collapse and with the ambiguity of a deity who calls a people his chosen community while at the same time destining it to annihilation. The difficult theological issues inherent in this profiling of God come to the fore in the confessional laments of the prophet as noted in Chapter 6 above. It is hard for Jeremiah to condemn his own people and hard that when he does utter this message God allows him to be badly treated as a result. Since the prophetic book is offered to communities of faith as a source of religious truth, any theological interpretation has to take account of the complex relations between God and justice which the work addresses.

One early study of the theological construction of Jeremiah was provided by Overholt (1970). He accepted the view that the book of Jeremiah breaks into layers of composition but sought for a theme which would be visible in multiple sections of material. In his book, Overholt holds on to a synchronic approach to the book of Jeremiah while acknowledging the individual subsections of material the work contains. He starts from the historical viewpoint of a real social environment existing in its last days before new political forces overthrow it but does not labour the details of this context. In this way, Overholt's study exemplifies some of the common issues involved in taking a theological approach to Jeremiah; these concern how far historical matters need to addressed, how far the autonomy of sections of the final text of Jeremiah should be respected and the relevance of attempting to take an over-arching cohesive approach to the nature and action of a given deity.

In carrying out his aim, Overholt took up the language of true and false prophecy which the book utilizes, noting that this has three strands: the false sense of security on the part of the people, false prophets and the falsehood of idolatry—all of them connected with the key term lie/falsehood. Using this reading lens, Overholt worked through Jeremiah identifying the variations on the common theme which appear in successive chapters, from the temple sermons of the prophet to conflicts with those depicted as false prophets to the lament passages such as Jer. 23.9-40. Overholt notes that on occasions Jeremiah's attitude to political rivals is ambiguous but that the overall theme of the text is to stress social isolation. The feeding into the Judahite culture of competing factional politics produces an actual separation from the deity. Wrong politics leads to wrong theology and thus to divine abandonment.

Overholt's diachronic/synchronic methods have been used extensively by one major player in the field of theological interpretation of Jeremiah for modern Christian audiences—Walter Brueggemann. He has engaged in a number of publications with the religious messages of Jeremiah and how they can validly be interpreted for modern readers who seek for a religious message for their own time and place. In his book on the theology of Jeremiah (2006), he sets out to give a clear account of the major aspects of the theology of the book. He begins by acknowledging the difficulties which this project faces on account of the findings of historical research which uses a diachronic approach to the book, referring to the way in which modern commentaries differ in their approach to viewing the prophetic book as a unity or as a collection of disparate units.

Whereas Holladay, for example, believes that a single historical prophet shaped the entire work across a number of phases in his career, Carroll argues that almost nothing can be deduced about any historical figure from the contents of the prophetic book. Brueggemann cites Stulman's work as sitting in the middle of these opposing views; the original layers of poetry are accompanied by prose material which offers a commentary on and explicates the meaning of, the original core ideas of the book. Brueggemann states that this is a good middle stance and adds two further pieces to this base: the need to take seriously the immense world crisis in geopolitics which the book stems from and addresses and the rooting of the explanatory material in Jeremiah in the Sinaitic tradition.

He then speaks to the other major feature noted by scholars, the dominance of Jeremiah himself in the prophetic text. Again he balances between extremes, that the picture is that of the historical figure or that there is nothing here but a later ideology imposed on the material in the form of a biographical account. The original man is now lost to view, he says, but the development of his persona stems from attention to the content of the earlier material and is a genuine gloss on those units in the light of later community experience. Brueggemann thus chooses to work within the frame of existing scholarship in order to draw out his understanding of the book's theology. This, he argues, is a theology of the incomparability of the deity. The book subordinates all events and all nations to the control of this single God via an imaginative rhetoric which creates a public religio-history.

Key images of this all-powerful deity are found in his Name, the Lord of Hosts (Yhwh Sabbaoth) and in the verb 'to stir' which is used in Jeremiah 51, for example, to show how foreign nations who do not serve this deity are nonetheless made into tools for his activity. God stirs up Babylon against Judah but a second wonder is found when the deity will stir up the nations to defeat Babylon itself. The same God both sides with his people and with their enemy, whom he uses but will discard. Jeremiah is part of this theology as God's special messenger. His profile is highlighted by minor characters such as Hananiah and Baruch. Hananiah means 'God is gracious' and he personifies a stable, supportive deity but this image is less than the divine truth, representing the human aspirations of the government elite for their own supremacy. Baruch in Jeremiah 45 functions as the agent of preservation of the Jeremiah tradition. In his association with the scroll and the emergence of a written tradition he is parallel with the Deuternomic model of Jeremiah as a Torah prophet, like Moses. The ultimate theological task of Jeremiah is to articulate the reality of Yhwh in a complex disputatious world crisis.

Brueggemann's treatment of the fragmented book of Jeremiah which allows for redactional activity in its compilation while seeking to preserve an overall continuity in the nature and purpose of the deity can be compared with the methods used by O'Connor in her essay (1999) referred to in Chapter 5 above. She too is aware of the difficulty of writing about the theology of the book when historical criticism has broken it into so many separate units but she does not try to synthesize the images of God found in Jeremiah in a direct manner. Instead, she discusses God as a fragmented persona, emerging from a fragmented book. She creates a theology which spotlights the non-unified, de-stabilized, multiple character of the deity by exploring the range of independent metaphors for God in the book. From this collection of divine icons, she suggests that there emerges a literary structure in which the image of divine tears radically deconstructs divine transcendence. God may be in charge but this is a deity whose characterization echoes the traumas of the people whom God has taken in charge.

Eric Peels' essay on the assassination of Gedaliah in Jeremiah 40–41 (2009) stands in between these two approaches in terms of aligning itself with historical and rhetorical approaches to religious message. Peels treats the countries and persons named in this passage as symbols within the rhetorical intention of Jeremiah, which is to promote reflection on the link between politics and divine intention, while at the same time accepting that the countries named had an historical profile. Egypt and Babylon, he states, are two theo-political entities in the prophetic book, while Gedaliah, Ishmael and Johanan stand for three stereotypical political viewpoints about relations with these two states.

Gedaliah stands for the political realism of submitting to Babylon in the present so as to preserve the kingdom for the future. Ishmael is the nationalist who works for independence at all costs, while Johanan dramatizes the voice of despair—the situation is so desperate that only Egypt can offer a way out. Peels comments on the theological message constructed by the textual rhetoric with reference to Brueggemann's approach to prophetic theology. At one level, Jeremiah is all about the politics of submission to Babylon in a problematic international situation; it is a pro-Babylonian propaganda piece. But on a further level, he suggests, the book moves from political ideology to pastoral sensitivity to the exile and from there to a daring theological view: namely, that faith in a deity is still a viable commitment even in a world setting which is falling apart.

Brueggemann's work on the religious meanings of Jeremiah offers a bridge between reading the prophetic book as a literal account of historical events and as a work of religious significance. It does this by drawing on the symbolism of the biblical text, an approach which Brueggemann took up before the full emergence of rhetorical criticism in its own right. In his two works, *The Prophetic Imagination* (1978) and *The Hopeful Imagination* (1986), he focused on the part played by imagination in shaping prophetic meaning. Imaginative acts allow the fears and hopes of human groups to be brought to public expression, he argues. The language of grief cuts through the complacent attitude of a royal elite, forming a Jeremiah who is an exemplar of pathos through his recognition of the political blindness of the leadership of his day. In the second of these books, Brueggemann dwells more on the character of Jeremiah and his role in articulating conflict. In this role, the prophet's speech is robust and challenging; God is an abandoned bridegroom, a lion, a wolf. The theological language of the book is free, porous and impressionistic which allows hope to emerge from the zero hour of loss and exile, as in Jer. 30.12-17.

Erhard Gerstenberger (2002) brings together a socio-economic approach to religious teaching with the biblical account of the history of social development of Israel provided in the Hebrew Bible. This approach allows him to acknowledge fully the diversity of theologies to be found in the biblical material, the many versions of who God is in relationship to the community systems of a given time setting. He moves back from the final layer of exclusive monotheism to the traces of earlier views still present in the final version of Israelite theology. He opts for a sociological approach to theological analysis, aligning each profile of God with a particular stage in political development. With regard to prophecy, he notes the tension between two stages of social change.

The times of the earlier kings, he suggests, indicate a state theology, a kingdom theology which united king and religion and produced a deity who served the interests of the kingdom, even though his perspective was occasionally challenged by dissident groups composed of those on the margins of society. In the times of written prophecy Gerstenberger sees a shift from the local state deity brought about by invasion and exile. He accounts for books such as that of Jeremiah within this framework of exilic theologies, which rested on the preservation of cultural identity through the creation of written materials, the scriptures. Being part of a wider empire could have caused the exiled Judahites to abandon the deity who had failed to protect them but the need to maintain their own traditional identity led the exiles to retain a belief in their ancestral deity, holding up the Name of the Lord as of continuing importance.

This approach can be found in Jer. 23.5-6, according to Gerstenberger, while the clash with the followers of the Queen of Heaven in Jer. 44.15-19 indicates that the need to preserve identity produced an impetus towards exclusive iconography of God. Jeremiah's theology is thus shaped by the conditions caused by demoralizing political changes, by new emphasis on the role of family in preserving a unique cultural identity and by an ambiguous interpretation of historical experience. These chronological realities eventually fired the emergence of a universalist stance with the local deity retained by demonstrating that this God is in fact in sole charge of all nations and their inter-related fortunes. The need to preserve the otherness of Judahite culture led to the concept of election being stressed, which in turn fed into a view of the exalted status of God alongside the holiness required of his people. Such a deity could be seen as sharing his people's sorrows, as in Jer. 31.20 and Jer. 4.19-22.

Reviewing these several versions of the theology of Jeremiah, it can be seen that a number of methods of reading have been at work among scholars. In all cases, the depiction of the character of God turns ultimately on the foundational interpretation of the text through historical and rhetorical criticism. Gerstenberger shares with O'Connor the concept of a suffering deity, one who feels their pain alongside them, even though the means by which these two scholars arrive at their viewpoint are not the same. Overholt, Peels and Brueggemann share the common style of measuring the rhetoric of Jeremiah against the known facts of radical political change dealt with in the biblical book. Brueggemann extends this level of interpretation to other experiences of state complacency and of political upheaval for which the book of Jeremiah offers tools for the production of a relevant religious message, including those in the modern world. In this way, he shares the concern of contextual theology which interests itself with the real life of readers but for him this can viably include live religious belief among modern worshippers.

The coverage given above to versions of biblical theology, as these emerge from reading the book of Jeremiah, highlight once again the basic fact that in Jeremiah readers find one book but many versions of what this book means and how it was shaped to express those meanings. History, narrative and theology are all valid labels which can be attached to Jeremiah and which share a common tradition of political experience during the rise to imperial status in the ancient Near East of neo-Assyria, Babylonia and Persia. With regard to Jeremiah's place within a collection of sacred books it is the theological angle which has determined the book's survival but theology is derived from underlying civil society's experience of statehood and of military defeat. History cannot be separated from theology, yet historical events are now found as part of a written story and time needs to be given to consider carefully the shape of the written materials.

Poetry, prose, metaphor and symbol are key literary devices which communicate the particular flavour of the book of Jeremiah as one permeated by the themes of terror, pain and loss. The story is not, however, set in a fantasy world which aims to be alien. Rather, it is the daily historical world of regional politics which provides the urge to produce a written account about a community which suffered and about those who survived to tell the tale. Although there are grave difficulties in accessing the details of historical events as they occurred, history in a wider sense forms the basis both for story and for theology. The writing of history—historiography—draws together specific events and the imparting to these separate occurrences of a generic purpose within the cosmos. Chance and randomness are replaced with control and intention as a theological overview is produced. The simple formula of 'the word of the Lord' provides events with a cause and thus with an explanation. By the creation of prose narratives, poetic material is provided with particular meaning. Oracles which appear to be the record of divine direct speech are thereby rooted in the community's traditions and contribute to its self-identity.

In these movements within Jeremiah theology, story and history work together as styles of cultural expression and individual passages can be read from more than one of these levels. Take, for example, the call narrative of Jeremiah 1, where the task of the prophet is said to be to pull down existing political structures, a message repeated in chap. 45. This motif can be read historically from the angle of prophetic insight into international relations of the time. Foreign invaders did indeed break down or tear up small local kingdoms they encountered on their path through alien territory. Questions can be asked as to who these invaders were, where they came from, their military campaigns and political styles.

The same motif gives life to the theological image of the prophet as one who brings about change through his speech-acts, in a performative utterance which enacts a legal prosecution of the government of Judah. This can be commented on both from the perspective of a literary genre and from that of what prophets were understood to be capable of in antiquity. The motif can, equally, be explored as a pair of matching bookends, chaps.

1–45, which start and end content which centres on the mood of terror and trauma, expressed both poetically and in plain prose. Finally, the theme of destruction may be examined under the concept of divine anger, leading to theological debate about theodicy and human guilt.

A second case study can be found in Jer. 20.7-12, a passage within the confessions genre. Historically examined, the words of pain and desperation in this poetic unit can be described as the real experience of a man whose task is to stand against the majority beliefs of his fellow elite. Read as a report from that historical prophet, the contents can be matched with prose scenes in which Jeremiah is thrown into prison or has his writings destroyed by the king. In this approach, the lament psalm of Jeremiah 20 is given cultural depth by biographical data. Read rhetorically, the unit offers a freestanding poetic interpretation of isolation, scapegoating and communal violence—actions and states which happen to human beings at large.

In this approach, the literary persona of Jeremiah provides a companion in sorrow for those in distress. In vv. 14-18 the cursing of one's birth provides a measure for grief which exceeds all normal bounds, finding its parallel in Job 3 where the patriarch Job has lost everything dear to him, surviving only with the breath still in his body. Theologically, the expression of such deep anxiety leads to debates about the justice of God, as it does in the discourses in the book of Job. Reading intertextually opens up the human mind to the vastness of transcendent space and the incapacity of the limited human mind to encompass absolute meaning and make sense of it.

Or one can take the scene where Jeremiah writes scrolls which he entrusts to his servant Baruch (Jer. 36.27-32). The scene which links prophet, scribe and scroll could be investigated as an example of scribal activity in the late monarchy, indicating the existence of a 'civil service' within the royal court in Judah. Baruch could also be read as an historical follower of the prophet who treasured his master's words until the time came that they were proved accurate and so current. Or, this scene could indicate a time when textual data began to move from oral memory to settled written formats. Or, Baruch can be read as an extra character, inserted into earlier material at a later date as a representative of later groups who wanted to show that their entitlement to office went back to past historical roots.

Yet again, Baruch, Jeremiah and the scroll can be examined as agents of the narrative plot of Jeremiah. In this reading style, attention is given to the literary construction of their character, their interaction in the passage and the way in which the inanimate written text gains a life within the story, becoming an agency by which the plot concerning the long-term survival of prophetic activity moves along. The line of tradition passes from the founder figure to his attendant and from that human being emerge the written materials which will make the tradition live across future generations. Jeremiah's message of political collapse and annihilation will achieve in this handing on process the status of timeless iconography of traumatic experience. In terms of theology, the scroll can be understood as the material equivalent of living divine utterance. When the scroll is read in the context of worship and study it acts as a form of divine agent, the site where divine presence tabernacles and which embodies the dynamism of transcendent power to change reality.

In this chapter, there has been a focus on scholarship which seeks to uncover and communicate a specifically transcendent aspect to the book of Jeremiah, but it has been demonstrated that biblical theology views the divine as operating within the time-space dimensions of human society. God is found within the events of daily life—in Jeremiah this means discovering the deity at work in international politics and in the violence of military aggression. Both poetry and prose are suitable media for communicating the prophetic voice making human language capable of carrying divine truth through metaphor and religious symbols.

By returning to an examination of the text of Jeremiah in the light of the history of interpretation provided by this introductory guide, the reader can continue the process of finding personal and social meaning in this ancient work of literature. There is great value in reading again the contents of Jeremiah and following up the first engagement with the text as set out in Chapter 2 above, this time pausing at each subunit of the book and considering what historical, literary and theological questions can be asked regarding that small part of the overall work. It can reasonably be said here that questions are even more important than answers as tools for investigating the book of Jeremiah at greater depth.

## Further Reading and References

Brueggemann, W.
    1978    *The Prophetic Imagination* (Philadelphia: Fortress Press).
    1986    *The Hopeful Imagination* (Philadelphia: Fortress Press).
    2006    *The Theology of the Book of Jeremiah* (Cambridge: Cambridge University Press).
Gerstenberger, E.
    2002    *Theologies in the Old Testament* (New York/London: T. & T. Clark International).
Overholt, T.
    1970    *The Threat of Falsehood: A Study in the Theology of the Book of Jeremiah* (London: SCM Press).
Peels, E.
    2009    'The Assassination of Gedaliah (Jeremiah 40:7–41:18)', in Bob Becking and Dirk J. Human (eds.), *Exile and Suffering* (Leiden: Brill), pp. 83-104.

# INDEXES

## INDEX OF REFERENCES

### OLD TESTAMENT

## INDEX OF AUTHORS